Margate in the early 19th Century was an exciting town, where smugglers and 'preventive men' fought to outwit each other, while artists such as JMW Turner came to paint the glorious sunsets over the sea. One of the young men growing up in this environment decided to set out for Australia to make his fortune in the Bendigo gold rush.

Half a century later, having become a pillar of the community, he began writing a series of letters and articles for Keble's Gazette, a publication based in his home town. In these, he described Margate with great familiarity (and tremendous powers of recall), while at the same time introducing his English readers to the "latitudinarian democracy" of a new, "young Britain".

Viney's interests covered a huge range of topics, from Thanet folk customs such as Hoodening, through diatribes on the perils of assigning intelligence to dogs, to geological theories including suggestions for the removal of sandbanks off the English coast "in obedience to the sovereign will and intelligence of man".

His writing is clearly that of a well-educated man, albeit with certain Victorian prejudices about the colonies that may make those with modern sensibilities wince a little. Yet above all, it is interesting because of the light it throws on life in a British seaside town some 180 years ago.

This book also contains numerous contemporary illustrations.

Turner's Margate through Contemporary Eyes

The Viney Letters

Compiled & edited by Stephen Channing

Turner's Margate Through Contemporary Eyes
The Viney Letters

Original texts by S.W. Viney et al.
Editorial additions © Stephen Channing 2009
Photograph of Hoodeners (page 44) reproduced by kind permission of the St Nicholas-at-Wade & Sarre Hoodeners
Portrait of S.W. Viney (page 69) reproduced by kind permission of the Pictures Collection, State Library of Victoria

Every reasonable effort was made to track down the copyright holders for all content used in this publication. Please contact us if you become aware of any copyrighted material used inappropriately.

All rights reserved. No part of this document may be reproduced, copied, distributed, transferred, modified, or transmitted, in any form or by any means, electronic or mechanical, including photocopying, recording, or by any information storage or retrieval system, without the prior written permission of the copyright owner; nor can it be circulated in any form of binding or cover other than that in which it is published and without similar conditions including this condition being imposed on a subsequent purchaser. In no event shall the author or publisher be liable for any damages caused in any way by use of this document.

Published by Ōzaru Books, an imprint of BJ Translations Ltd
Street Acre, St Nicholas-at-Wade, BIRCHINGTON, CT7 0NG, U.K.
https://ozaru.net/ozarubooks

First edition published December 2009 (minor revisions made in 2023)
ISBN: 978-0-9559219-2-6

CONTENTS

List of Illustrations ix
Introduction 1
Recollections of Margate, Half a Century Since 5
    Shipwrecks, vendors, boat builders, bathing rooms 5
    Hoodening, accidents, dancing, theatre, lawyers, doctors, schools, regatta .. 17
    Ghosts, contraband, entertainers, drinks, games 29
    Tea gardens, Boulevard, donkeys 36
    Children's games, chalk, packets & steamships, art 39
    Passenger boats, cross-channel trade, paintings 41
Responses to Viney's Recollections 44
    The "Hooden Horse" 44
    "Ye Haunted House" 45
Jottings From Australia 46
    Dealing with lazy *émigrés*, Ly-ee-moon shipwreck 46
    Charity performances, showmen, carnival, New Guinea, lost wreck .. 48
    A Chapter About Dogs 49
    The Goodwins 51
    Response from Mid-Kent 54
    In Jest 55
    Ryan's riposte 56
    Sand banks – their origins, uses and demolition 56
    The Brake Sand 58
    Volcanoes, glaciers and icebergs 59
    Alcohol, elections, memorial poems 60
    Democracy, bishop, cricket, politicians 61
    Election, shipwreck, gold rush, seismic activity 63
The vicar's poem 65
The Margate Crier: Thomas "Toby" Philpot 68
Stewart Warrender Viney 69
    Viney and Turner 73
    Sources 75
Index of names, places and topics 77

List of Illustrations

1821 map of Margate 4
Margate Harbour from the sea, c. 1825 5
No Man's Land 6
High Street and Garner's Library 7
Old Droit office 8
New Droit office and Jarvis's Landing Place 8
Marine Parade 9
Old Iron Bridge and lighthouse, c. 1835 9
King Street Bridge 10
High Street & Queen Street 11
High Street & front of Bathing Houses (low buildings on the left) 12
Cold Harbour 13
View from the Gallery of Garner's Library 14
Gambling scene 14
Bettison's Library in Hawley Square 15
Interior of Bettison's Library 16
Road Leading to the Fort 18
Newgate and the preventive station 19
Steam boats leaving Margate 20
The Jetty Head 20
Tivoli Gardens 21
View from the Fort 23
Theatre Royal 24
Buenos Ayres, with the Prevention Post 25
Gloucester Lodge 26
Dane Hill House Academy 27
Margate regatta 28
Site of the 1832 Reform Bill fiasco 29
Cranbourne Alley 30
Marine Terrace 31
The Assembly Rooms and Royal Hotel, Cecil Square 32
Royal Hotel exterior from the other side 32
Assembly Rooms interior 33

The back of the Bathing Houses 34
Cobb's Brewery. Taken near the Fort 35
The Boulevard in 1832 37
Ranelagh Tea Gardens in St Peter's 37
Donkey people 39
Steam packet arriving in Margate 42
The Harlequin at Margate Pier 43
Early 20th century Hoodeners with their Horse 44
Margate Harbour by Turner (1824) 74
Sunrise – Whiting Fishing off Margate by Turner (1834) 74

Introduction

While engaged in research in Margate's Library, I happened across an article in an edition of a weekly newspaper called "Keble's Gazette"entitled "Recollections of Margate". Being thus distracted from my original research, further searching revealed that these recollections had been published in "Keble's Gazette" randomly over a space of nearly four years. As an historian who has studied local history at degree level I knew straight away that this kind of historical source is very rare, but what makes this particular source even more special is that the narrator has a great sense of humour combined with intellectual brilliance.

The contents of this resultant publication have, to my knowledge, never been published in book form and, as far as I am aware, have not seen the light of day since the last instalment was published in a column of the "Keble's Gazette" in 1886, the first being printed in 1882.

It was from Bendigo (at the time named Sandhurst) near Melbourne, Australia that Stewart Warrender Viney wrote his recollections of Margate in the 1820s and 1830s, for the entertainment of the readers of Keble's Gazette in Kent, England.

Stewart Warrender Viney was evidently a very educated man as his recollections of Margate portray great eloquence and wit, along with an ability to recall names and places, even after more than fifty years had elapsed, making this book, in my opinion, an historical gem. His often humorous insight into every day life in Margate nearly two hundred years ago not only provides a wealth of information for the local historian but flows like a novel where people, places, sights and smells come alive. In Viney's obituary in "The Bendigo Advertiser" on 4 May 1897 Viney is portrayed as "...being possessed of considerable literary ability..."

Amongst his recollections Viney talks about – "playing in front of the old droit office without clock tower" – and the original lighthouse – "...a little octagon-shaped wooden erection which always suggested to my childish fancy a bottle washing jack....". He also recollects the first steamboats and the demise of old sailing ships such as "The Margate Hoy" which was "run off" the roads in about 1822-3, and mentions such detail as:

> "...I see a stout-built round-sterned obese kind of ark, with carved rudder head and ancient tiller, the White Horse and "Invicta" prominent thereon. This is the Hoy "Thanet," of which Captain Malpas, a portly weather-beaten man, is present Commander..."

Also revealed in the recollections are details of Margate's first regatta of 1828, and of when he attended "...one of the old fashioned quality balls at the old Assembly Rooms...". He wrote of incidents at "Tivoli Gardens" and naughty goings-on at the "Theatre Royal" when he was just a young boy. Viney also gives us an account of the time he worked for Mr John Boys the solicitor. Mentioned in detail is Margate's appalling open-air celebration of 1832 following the passing of the Reform Bill, plus lots about ghosts and smuggling. The last date referred to in his recollections of Margate is 1838.

All in all, I found the information in Viney's recollections fascinating and very informative with mention of over eighty different local family names. It is so rare to find documents of this nature, especially one so detailed and depictive of a period so long ago, that it deserves to be published for all to enjoy.

Although the text of this book is verbatim I have decided to include contemporary illustrations of some of the places that the narrator describes, so as to create a "visual" understanding when reading this book. One can easily become confused about streets and other locations because Margate has changed so much over the years and I believe the illustrations help provide another dimension to Viney's descriptions, that otherwise so vividly describe places that no longer exist. As well as trying to explain where these places were I have also tried to identify what now occupies their place.

At the end of this book I have included other writings by Viney that had been sent to Keble's Gazette for "the entertainment of Margate's readers", for they give an insight into his life during the early colonisation of Australia and his personal memories of Bendigo, its development and its people, many of whom had also left The Isle of Thanet for Australia in the 1840s and 50s.

The contents of this book will no doubt offer a significant resource for local historians and genealogists for not only does it contain many names and descriptions of local characters, it gives a very detailed first hand account of what it was like living in Margate around the harbour area in the 1820s and 30s. Enjoy.

S. M. Channing

Acknowledgements

My thanks go to the following:

- Margate Library for allowing me to copy their 1821 town map of Margate and numerous other prints and engravings for use in this book, and for supplying access to Keble's Gazette
- Australia's Victoria State Library for granting permission to include archive materials, including the only known photograph of Stewart Warrender Viney
- The Goldfields Library Corporation in Bendigo, for sharing Viney's obituary, details of his family and extracts from the 1859 annals of Bendigo, Cemetery Query Report, Bendigo Rates Report, Bendigo Advertiser and Digger
- Finally, thanks to my wife Shirley for her patience and help in correcting my much-to-be-desired syntax

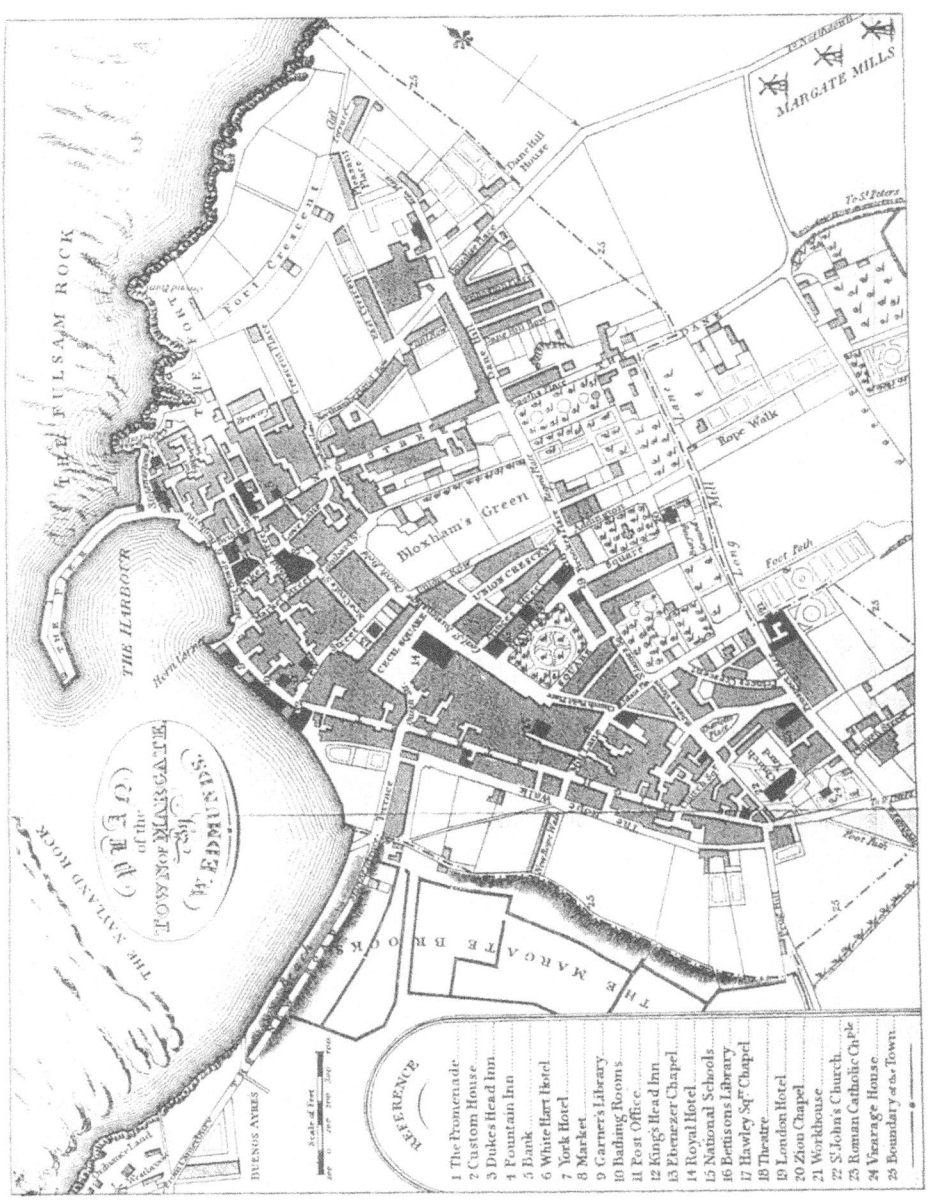

1821 map of Margate

Recollections of Margate, Half a Century Since

Shipwrecks, vendors, boat builders, bathing rooms

It may be a matter of speculation why I, with half a world in space and half a century in date between myself and an early residence in Margate as many years since, should feel fit to inflict my reminiscences on the present generation resident on that portion of Thanet's Isle, and possibly some brief explanation is almost demanded of me. Well, when a dear cousin, long resident in America (with whom I have for years maintained a close correspondence), paid a visit to the old country – prompted pretty much by similar motives to those which took Aeneas to the tomb of Anchises – and while at "home" he kindly forwarded me a photo taken from Margate Jetty Head (Jarvis's Jetty in my time), and musing over the view of the old town presented, many old memories welled up, and it occurred to me subsequently that possibly a retrospect of some of the old faces, places, and incidents might be pleasant to any old "standards," and even refreshing, for the sake of comparison to the younger, later denizens.

Margate Harbour from the sea, c. 1825

The Margate of those days was of protean character – five or six months of the year it was little but tearing winds and "going off" in boats to ships in distress; with now and again a shipwreck of more or less sensational character, the average resident, not engaged in marine business, hibernating pretty much after the fashion of the bears, and, like the Ursines, occupying himself in licking his paws, but as the summer solstice commenced, there was a general smell of green paint (a Margate man seemed to have a craze for green paint and used it incongruously and anaesthetically in everything from shutters to boats) observable, the women shook themselves together and rubbed, scrubbed, and furbished up everything capable of being scoured, and by the time the season was just comfortably aired by the north coming sun, Margate was one vast "Lodgings to let," and the arrival of the "boats" – for this was long anterior to railway connection with the metropolis – was looked for with much interest, and the unfortunate Cockneys – I don't use the term disparagingly, but as the vernacular of the period – who arrived were pounced upon, swooped upon, set upon – or any term which signifies actual appropriation – by the "touters," and their belongings taken violent possession of by "the ticket porter," and as the human was generally dragged away to the Fort, some of his or her family smuggled off down the Dane, and the chattel property of the family carefully deposited at Buenos Ayres, it was probably about midnight before a satisfactory reunion of the scattered entities was effected.

The sea-side lodging house keeper has been too much scarified by writers generally for me to throw another stone at them; they have their living to get in six months for the whole year, and if some little mysteries are connected with lodging house experience – well, it affords incident to recollection to be funny over afterwards.

I have wandered away from the old jetty head, however, and retrace my steps in front of me in lieu of the old No Man's Land, and first and second points, is a retaining wall – a sea wall surmounted by a grander hotel.

No Man's Land

This area, to the right of the harbour, was known as Fort Point. It is shown on the map on page 4 as being part of the mainland at the time. Today, the chalk "island" no longer exists, having been claimed by the gradual erosion of the sea.

The old Custom House remains, but has lost its official character. Cold Harbour, once the abode of a colony of washerwomen, who seemed to be ever in an atmosphere of reeking suds, appears an almost "select" place of residence, while by the aid of a microscopic glass I learn from the sign that "The Foy Boat, by W. Hudson," immortalised by Barham (Ingoldsby), is "The Foy" no longer, but a huge hotel ever-so many storeys high has taken the place of the unpretentious low-roofed pub of my time, and welcomes visitors under the name of the Pier Hotel. Still, I question if the malt purveyed in the newer edifice is equal to the Cobb's Entire of long, long ago. The Duke's Head still remains unchanged, but where is the genial James McAdams?

High Street and Garner's Library

The house on the left with the bow-fronted window is Ingoldsby House and is where Barham wrote the Ingoldsby Legends. It still remains today but the frontage has been altered. Garner's library on the right has since disappeared and has been replaced with the Imperial Hotel, which today has been modernised, providing luxury apartments and a wine bar.

The Droit Office is not the old building, without clock tower, in the front of which we boys used to play, and probably few will remember the original lighthouse, a little octagon-shaped wooden erection which always suggested to my childish fancy a bottle washing jack.

An incident of the new Droit Office presents itself to my mind. On the first occasion of lighting the illuminated clock in the tower, the old man (name forgotten) who was deputed to do so, incautiously allowed the gas to escape, and on his going up with a light the four clock faces were sent to the cardinal compass points they severally faced, and the custodian was picked up somewhat astonished, as were Messrs. S. S. Chancellor and Draper, the then Pier officers.

Another view, by the bye, shows me that neither local enterprise nor engineering constructiveness have yet thought of utilising the Nayland Rocks whereon to build a marine terrace walk, and form a protective wing to the harbour.

Old Droit office

New Droit office and Jarvis's Landing Place

These two pictures indicate the changes that Viney witnessed as a young boy. First, the old lighthouse shown in the top picture, that Viney remembers as "a little octagon-shaped wooden erection" was replaced by the stone one during the 1820s. The Droit House, built in 1812, also changed when an illuminated clock was added: Viney mentions an incident which saw the "...four clock faces sent to the cardinal compass points they severally faced..." when they were first lit up and exploded. Also notice the addition of Jarvis's Landing Jetty, built in 1824.

Marine Parade

The Lower Marine Parade remains unaltered – even by a coat of paint – and that delightful semi-circular arch iron bridge is still there to slip up and discomfit unwary persons.

Old Iron Bridge and lighthouse, c. 1835

This bridge was described by Viney as 'delightful', but was later levelled to create underground toilets near the current clock tower.

King Street Bridge

The cut between the houses in the above picture was created to allow a tidal inlet, known as the Creek, to flow through Dane Valley into the harbour, with a bridge built across it to allow access between Marine Parade and the Fort. It was probably filled in after the great storm of 1808. Today, the inlet is incorporated into the drainage system so allowing a proper thoroughfare called King Street to be built.

Of the people, the *dramatis personae*, so to speak, of the time, I must jot them down as they memorially stalk before me. The name of Dixon, Jemmy Dixon, seems to attach to a party who appears to me have been a pretty generally all-round man, into everything, and invested with ubiquity enough to be almost everywhere at once. Amongst the notables of the time, I after a pause remember Charley Forster, who dealt in coals and coffins, who was everywhere and in everything, and let nobody die in peace, almost insisting on an order for the last suit before the breath was out of the body. Then I hear during the morning hours, the bellman Philpott – reverently, but not necessarily baptismally, Toby – who rings a large bell and "cries" some lost property, the various entertainments for the evening, and informs the visitors that every accommodation is provided for them "at the tea gardens at Shallows at 1s per head, 8d if you bring your own tea and sugar, half-price for children," ending with a sonorous "God save the King!" followed by the general addition by some juvenile humorist, "And hang the Crier," and so he takes his yellow selvaged three-cornered hat and official coat off the scene; Billy Stokes, a gaunt lanthorn jawed vendor of lollipops, with a tin tray, scales, &c., slung before him, comes on, and in a shrill treble pipes out, looking most simple and lackadaisical, doggerel, something to this effect:

My ciniment and pepiment and sugar so nice,
Ony vun penny, ony vun penny;
Ony vun penny, so low is the price,
That if you buy vunce you'll buy twice in a trice.
Ony vun penny.

Another tinkling bell heralds the approach of a very cross-jack-eyed street merchant, named Waghorn, who in a loud blustering voice inquires whether there are purchasers for "a plum or seed cake."

Wandering up High Street through that narrowest and most dangerous point above the bathing rooms, I wander past John Bayly's well-known grocery shop, and the Elephant and Castle, by a printer's shop, a chemist and tooth-jerker's (my chamber of horrors where I was martyred out of several masticators by forceps, keys, and other instruments of torture), into Hawley Square and under the Piazza of the old Royal Hotel, where by-the-bye the elder Mathews[1], the first and perhaps the best of monopolylogists, used unaided to give his conversazione; behind the door below stood a remnant of a still further back era, "a sedan chair" with its poles proper for the bearers; whether it was ever used in those days your deponent saith not.

High Street & Queen Street

The above picture shows the site of "John Bayly's well known grocery shop," on the corner where now stands Boots the chemist. On the right you can just make out a part of the Elephant and Castle pub which was demolished in the 1970s.

---

[1] Charles Mathews (1776-1835), an actor well known for mimicry

High Street & front of Bathing Houses (low buildings on the left)

The large building at the bottom of the road on the left is Garner's library with its dome, where now stands the Imperial Hotel. The other side of the bathing houses lead directly onto the beach. You can see the harbour area in the background on the left.

Coming back to the sea margin, old associations are strong, and I, living down by the sea, was a beach boy; my very nose wakes up its memories, and I sniff on boiling-down days at Old Salter's Soap and Candle Works on Bankside, going up to Pump-Lane stiff, but combined with the aroma of decaying marine vegetation, and the harbour mud was not much behind Cologne. No doubt, however, that sanitary regulations have improved Old Salter and his vats off the face of Bankside.

Higher up a narrow and impossibly crooked street past Stranack's shop and residence, who by-the-bye imported in the old [ship] "Countess of Elgin" from Ostend, turkeys, fowls, rabbits, butter, eggs, walnuts, and Flemish wooden shoes, I came to Gore's boat building yard; they were wont to build large vessels fifty or sixty tons up there; notably the Big Kitty, which being brought down the hill "fetched away," and cut the corner of a house off.

A fellow feeling makes one wondrous kind, and I must not forget the donkeys; they were the delight of the Londoners, and male and female, young and old, went for donkey riding generally in groups of two or three with a youth following up the pace by leathering away at any laggards; the number of ladies – well females – who took asinine exercise gave rise to the following by some poetaster of the time, this may not be the actual text, but it is something like this:

> When Balaam swore his wicked vow,
> An Angel barred the way,
> But donkeys pass through Thanet now
> With Angels every day.

I don't know if the local society for the prevention of cruelty to animals has put a check on the "threshing machines," which the donkey boys were; if not it is time they did.

Cold Harbour

This picture shows the area near the jetty where Viney lived and spent a lot of his time playing when a young boy, although the buildings in this late Victorian photograph did not exist at that time. The building on the far right is part of the old Pier Hotel, which was demolished together with other old buildings in the Cold Harbour area in the 1930s, to make way for a new road. Later, in the 1960s, a pub called the Ship Inn was built but again improvements caused its demolition, followed by the construction of the current lifeboat station (the previous one having been part of the jetty, which collapsed during the storms of 1978). As this book goes to press, Turner Contemporary – a controversial yet exciting project that will surely put Margate back on the map – is being built on this site, where both Turner and Viney used to live.

Standing in my mind's eye, at the then stronghold of donkeydom, at the commencement of Lower Marine Terrace, I look up to a terrace, which I knew as Lansell's Terrace[2]; one of the family, George[3], is one of our quartz millionaires – ever so rich – by-the-bye another Margatonian – a lady this time – daughter of a rope maker, who twisted yarns at the walk behind the Jolly Sailor, is wife of our lucky miners, JB Watson; I don't know how much he's worth, questionable if he knows himself.

---

[2] probably later renamed Albert Terrace in memory of Queen Victoria's consort
[3] b. Margate 1823, emigrated 1853, accumulated 38 quartz & gold mines, d. Bendigo 1906

View from the Gallery of Garner's Library

Gambling scene

This is what Viney discusses in detail from his recollections of when he visited these establishments.

However, jumping back from Bendigo (Sandhurst) here to Margate there, I go in the evening first to the free concerts at the Bathing rooms, but as of a warm summer's evening, the not too well ventilated and closely packed rooms are stuffy, I stand a chance of an involuntary vapour bath; I head for the libraries where everything is bright and charming, a little music, a little singing, and a good deal of gambling, and a constant rattle of the dicing box, and cries of "only one wanting," simple *rationale*; each of four subscribe 6d, throw out dice, highest receives a ticket for 2s value, to be taken out on the establishment, and as all articles are ticketed at about 200 per cent above their extreme value, it is not a bad thing for the Garners and Bettisons, who race their affairs, and it is effective in getting rid of the young Thirtibobaweek's surplus cash.

Bettison's Library in Hawley Square
Standing on this site now is Hilderstone Adult Education Centre.

Besides the libraries there were bazaars for the lounger, and those who had spare cash, one Levy's Boulevard, a narrow corridor, having a dark passage through into Hawley Square, the walls covered with flaring paper, illustrative of the French war in the East, here amid a pleasant Frenchy smell of scented soap and pastilles, musical boxes grinding out popular music, along the sides were stalls of toys and nic-nacery of various kind. Then came Jolly's bazaar, an annex to a large drapery establishment in High Street, and then the London bazaar at the back of High Street, which was still less Frenchy, and more on the lines of the famed Soho bazaar in London.

There was a weakness of the newly arrived Londoner which I recollect, and which doubtless put many a guinea into the pockets of Drs Price, Waddington, and other practitioners, viz., hot pork pie for supper, a horribly nightmarey food at best, and sometimes on the top of a good deal of liquid refreshment and cigars, productive of acute colic in the night.

Interior of Bettison's Library

And now my thought takes me up a flight of break-neck steps near the Custom House, to a little row of cottages on the brow of the cliff, looking out to the sea, that is from the back – the front giving on a little quadrangular grass plot, Britannia – or was it Alfred Square, surrounded by sail makers' lofts, boat builder's shops, &c. I do remember me of a stately lady of quality, Lady Elliott I think, who yearly took up her abode here and was for her stay the cynosure of wandering eyes in that locality, from her quaint style of dress and ancient jewellery, a sort of, cross in my imagination between *Marie Antoinette*, and Hannah Moore, as I knew those celebrities from pictures, whether the old Dowager loved the simple life, associated with the fisher folk, or was economically retrenching after the dissipation of the London season, I know not.

I don't know whether as in other things time has adjusted demand and supply in the matter of horses, but in those days Margate was the great post of entry for Flemish horses, and it was one of the boy sights to go down the pier and see the animals hoisted up; another very popular cargo which was wont to arrive, were cargoes of apples in bulk from the Channel Islands, Guernsey, &c., and youth had a good time on those occasions. And now I fear I have already trespassed in my *cacoethes scribendi* of your space and patience, although as I go on still more and more recollections well up in my memory, but enough for the present.

Hoodening, accidents, dancing, theatre, lawyers, doctors, schools, regatta

There may be in the few memorial incidents which I send you, something to interest your readers. One of my earliest recollections is of an institution long enough discontinued to be forgotten, save an old fogey like myself, for I believe the custom has not been observed since 1824-5. It was the practice about Christmas time – either Christmas Eve or Twelfth Night – for a band of young fellows to go "a hoodening." That is, each being somewhat disguised, and bearing a long staff or broom-stick, they brought round one of their party, whose head was enveloped in rude imitation of a horse's head, with a mechanical lower jaw, and painted with large goggle eyes, red lips, and big teeth, which was enough in its entirety of ugliness to afford a good basis for a general nightmare. The party, as I have described it, formed a semi-circle round a door, the "horse" being in the centre; they then chanted some rude jargon (which my memory fails to furnish, if it was ever intelligible), stamping their staves in tune; on the door being opened and "largess" demanded, the "horse" was wont to gnash his teeth in a very dreadful nature, much to the fright of the servant and the children of the family, who clung to her, and peeped round her skirts at the appalling spectacle. The proceeds of this blackmailing, I assume, went in refreshments for the "hoodeners."

It is a somewhat significant fact and corroborative of the idea that the Welsh originally occupied the South-Eastern part of England and were gradually driven back by invaders till they gained safety in their own fastnesses that they have, or had till lately, a similar institution, under the more poetical name of "Mary Lloyd." Although it has nothing to do with the custom I have described, I find that a clothes basket, called in East Kent a "flasket," bears the same name in Wales, which in no other part of great Britain would that name apply to such a piece of wicker work. As to the origin of "hoodening," archaeologists might work it out, when we consider Hooden as a perversion of Odin or Woden, and the horse's head the familiar sign of the Scandinavian or Dane, who landed from time to time on the Kentish coast; and which is still preserved in the white horse of Kent. The custom itself – one more honoured now in the breach than the observance – was suppressed about the date above named, in consequence of a woman I think at St Lawrence, being thereby frightened to death.

I remember a gun being on "The Fort." But this was removed, I suppose, about 1825-6; but, singular enough, from one of the "Margate views" sent me, I see another gun in somewhat the same position. The present one is, I believe, one of the Russian cannons from the war of 1855 I presume, a relic from Sebastopol.

The hailstorm of the autumn of 1833, which occurred about September, will be in the memory of the "oldest inhabitants," I dare say. The back windows of the entire Upper and Lower Marine Terrace were broken to within a small percentage, and many other parts of the town suffered, notably the glass in the dome of Bettison's Library in Cecil Square. The glaziers had a merry time of it, the demands exceeding the supply so far that oiled paper "was your only ware" for many a day. Occurring as it did at night, and accompanied by heavy thunder and lightening, the storm caused a great deal of alarm.

Road Leading to the Fort

The building on the left in the picture above is the Custom House. The one on the right, with its two bay windows, is where the artist JMW Turner stayed with Mrs Booth during the 1820s-40s. The beach shown in the illustration was then known as "Little Beach." It has now been in-filled and is utilised as a car park. The little bit of a building that can just be made out on the far right was the "Foy Boat" pub that Viney recalls as "the unpretentious low-roofed pub of my time."

In those days the catch of sprats, generally somewhat undersize, would be so excessive that they were often sold by the bushel (4d, I think) to the farmers for manure, the indigent being allowed to pick out as many sizable ones as they pleased, for cooking.

I don't know whether Margate maintains its prolific character, but I remember once seeing a dish literally of little humans – four – which were exhibited (being covered with a roughly made glass case) at 6d a head – that is the spectator's not the children's.

Many of the present residents will, walking past the Newgate, at the first Preventive Station, east of the town, be unaware of that same cleft in the cliff having being the scene of a sad episode; a rail protects, or did protect, the passenger from falling or walking into the gap way, and one summer's evening one of the Preventive Service men was dancing the officer's baby child in the air while leaning against this rail. The child went further than the man calculated, and coming down over balanced them into the chasm. Both were killed on the spot. They are buried together in St John's churchyard.

Newgate and the preventive station

This gap is situated in the Cliftonville area of Margate, at the seaward end of Sweyn Road. A bridge, built in 2003, now spans the gap. This modern bridge replaced that built by Captain Frederick Hodges in 1861. Newgate Gap gives access to Walpole Bay.

There was a "pub" at that period that rejoiced in the name of "The Margate Hoy," on Bankside, and probably the gallant old ship which was the origin of the sign has long ere fulfilled the law of change, and gone up in smoke to make food for other trees, to build other ships, &c. She was a round-about serving mallet of a vessel, and, like her commander – one Malpas – was about as broad as she was long; a vessel from which the passenger would threaten to "get out and push behind." Yet this was the craft in which many hundreds of cocknies voyaged in – certainly justifying Froissart's idea that "we English take our pleasure sadly" – during their summerings at Margate. She however was, about 1822-3, run off the road as a passenger boat by the steam-boats Eclipse, Dart, Albion, and Magnet, later by the Royal George, William, and Adelaide, then the Herne, &c. up to the fine boats of the present, which are described to me. The Jetty – Jarvis's landing place – then became a necessity, and was the prototype of the present structure.

Engineering talent had not developed to the extent it has in later years, and the old construction "dipped" in the middle, so that unobservant persons – notably foolish young "spoons," who thought of nothing but of each other, whose "two hearts, which beat as one," – were often "nipped" on the jetty-head, and the gallant swain had to take up a lovely burden and wade through, amidst the laughter of the more thoughtful, or to hire a boat to reach *terra firma*.

Steam boats leaving Margate

Note the many small boats used to ferry passengers to and from the steamers, which could not enter the harbour at low tide.

The Jetty Head

Evidently this picture was simply updated after the building in 1824 of Jarvis's Landing Place. The jetty was mentioned on a number of occasions by Viney, generally to depict humorous incidents. Notice the huge chimneys on the early steamboats: it appears that they did not yet fully trust the new steam technology, as they still sported masts with sails. I wonder if they had oars tucked away somewhere as well!

"Out on the rocks" is a popular song of the period, but the prosaic realisation when caught and insulated by the incoming tide was a joke only to those on the mainland, while to those who had to wade in to the shore the thing was funny enough too, but unfortunately the fun was all on one side.

Memory takes me wandering down towards the Dane, and I see an old forge nearly opposite Cobb's Bank in which – the forge of course – the incandescent sparks seemed always to have been flying off the anvil. They are gone now; I suppose to make room for a more imposing edifice of some kind. Then there was an all-sorts shop – Mrs Arnsell, I think, was the presiding deity – where every thing that boyhood loves, or loved, were sold – tinsel for illuminating theatrical characters, cakes, bulls-eyes, a fearful preparation of boiled sugar made tastier with peppermint, fruits of various kinds, and, above all, as it presents itself to my memory's palate, "scorched peas." I have since then sat at good men's feasts, have eaten of the delicacies of almost every portion of the globe, but still all depraved as the taste may be, give me ye gods but one small tin measure – a halfpenny the price, I fancy – of Mrs Arnsell's "scorched peas," and leave me nothing to desire.

Tivoli Gardens

There is today very little visible evidence of where Tivoli Gardens existed. A few bits of low wall near the tennis courts in Tivoli Park Avenue, close to the old railway bridge, is what is left of the grand entrance to Tivoli, which one would have seen on disembarking from the early Victorian railway station, which stood on the now defunct railway line nearby. The rest of Tivoli Gardens would have stretched over the road into what is now Hartsdown Park.

In those days there were tea gardens – "shallows" (referred to before), and "shady groves" which blossomed and bloomed into "Tivoli," with song, melodramatic entertainments, fireworks, and dancing. Here poor Herr von Joel, the ventriloquist the *siffleur* and first Jodel-ler, introduced his imitations of birds and animals and his "Lurliety" jodel, which was affected by the best youth of the day – in the streets by night – till lurl-li-li-e-tee with its repetitions and variations became almost monotonous.

An incident connected with this place occurs to me, which verifies the much hackneyed *tempora mutantur*; about 1838 the gardens (Tivoli) were open in the evening for a dance the company being respectable but "mixed" and certainly not too punctilious about the proprieties. Amongst others threat disporting was one of the young Lushingtons, a son of one of the then country members – with a *chère amie* from Paris. This couple discarding the *noli me tangere* style of waltz, then in vogue, gyrated in a close embrace as is common at the present time and is not held to be indecorous or improper; the crowd, however, partly from envy at the graceful illustration of the poetry of motion which they had not been educated up to, and partly from an idea that the proprieties had been outraged, made such a fuss and were so virtuously indignant that poor Lushington and the lady would have been roughly handled had not myself and some others formed a sort of bodyguard or protectorate and smuggled them through "The Falls of Schaffsneesin" which formed the drop scene of the little proscenium of the stage. I am confident that these people were guilty of no more impropriety of conduct than may be seen in any well-conducted ballroom of the present.

Coming back to Margate proper, my mind's eye settles on a brick-built tenement two or three stories high at the corner of Cold-Harbour, next to the Pier Hotel – "Whilom, the Foy Boat, by W. Hudson." This side is familiar to me as occupied by a large barn of a building of most primitive construction; wood framing, coated and brick-nogged with roughest of materials, without windows seaward or, as I recollect, many lights anywhere save at the front door, which was of glass. I am particular about the house because it was the home of a boy who should have come up and made his mark as a hero. One Jerry (possibly Jeremiah) Doughty, who was born with that facial disfigurement an hare-lip, and over-hearing that there were great doctors in London who could cure it, actually when only aged about nine or ten slipped on board one of the steam boats leaving for London; asked his way about London till he happened to meet with a medical man, who hearing his story and admiring the boldness of the boy, performed the operation, and Jerry returned home in a day or two in a fair way to a permanent cure.

Strange how the mental presence of that locality calls up a troop of Emptages, Jenkinses, Maxteds, Braziers, Harmans – one "shug of that ilk" – Sandwells, Hubbards, Bartletts, Foxes, Rowes, and others. Poor old Jennings, happy on two wooden legs, his own being snapped off on board the Margate Hoy before referred to.

They were mostly tubby boats in those days, except indeed the galley boats which were fleet enough; there were few yachts visiting the port, and perhaps the smartest thing on the coast was the revenue cutter, Skylark, Capt. Quested, the terror of the contrabandists.

View from the Fort

I wonder if the solitary building, middle left is the "large barn of a building of most primitive construction," mentioned by Viney?

Going up a flight of stairs then existent between the Foy and Mrs Doughty's, which were, or should have been named Breakneck-stairs, with a little *detour* past Stranack's corner, one got amongst boat builders, sail makers, and herring-hangs, the air became redolent of pitch, tar, green paint – green paint ever in the ascendant – dried fish, salt-water, and seaweed in one delightful *mélange*. I have also a vision of a passage from High Street going out on the stone retaining wall leading to Lower Marine Terrace; it seems to me at this distance of time that this was the very "temple of the winds," and from whatever quarter it blew it always tore through there fit to tear your hair off or blow your teeth down your throat, and in the winter time, if my memory serves me it *can* blow sometimes in Margate.

There was at one time an attempt to make the Russian mountains [4] an entertainment at Margate, and they ran for a short time, the *locale* being in some fields out beyond Zion Chapel; whether they, however, did not come up to Bob Fudge's description [5] – "I've tried all these mountains, Swiss, French, and Ruggieri's, and think for digestion there's none like the Russian," or whether the doctors of the period, who were mighty autocratic, finding them too provocative of health, ordered them off, this deponent saith not; they went and left no mark.

The Theatre, too, as it seems to be common to all Theatres, stood in the queerest of all queer localities on the high road to no where. I have a remembrance of a day light visit to the interior by virtue of a fellowship with the boys of the purveyor of "apples, oranges, biscuits, or a bill of the play;" it presents itself as dirtier and dingier amongst the scenes than some I have visited in later years. Here the Savilles

---

[4] roller coasters

[5] in Thomas Moore's The Fudge Family in Paris (pub. 1818)

and Vinings were wont to "strut their hour," and some artistes who subsequently obtained eminence in the profession made early appearances; here poor old Sibbald, I think, was the *primo* in the orchestra. His was an imposing presence – especially looking down at the back of a very bald, shiny, ostrich-egg looking head – and as the war correspondents say, "drew down the fire of the enemy," for a very improper young scapegrace named Crow, with a well-directed shot with crab apple (taken in, I fear, purposely for this nefarious purpose), landed bang on the maestro's head and ricocheted across the stage. Youth *will* be youth, you know, but it was very improper. Bob Crow was full of fun, that's a fact.

Theatre Royal

This is how the old theatre looked when built in 1786. At the time our narrator visited it, it was only some 30 or 40 years old.

Smuggling was carried on largely at that period thanks to the heavy differential duties imposed; the devices of the contraband traders were many, and ingenious were the schemes to "run" either cargoes or small consignments, but I always entertained a belief that a judicious application of "golden ointment" was the best, easiest, and most popular mode. The preventative service, however, kept a good "look-out" from the cliff, and every load of seaweed (brought up for manure) was duly prodded with a long iron piercer for concealed seekers of spirits, parcels of tobacco, or other dutiable goods; but somehow, in spite of the coast *douaniers*, a large quantity of goods *did* escape and come into consumption, and so used were the people to smuggled productions that I have in my memory persons who would have no liquor in the house unless smuggled.

Buenos Ayres, with the Prevention Post
On this spot now stands the Nayland Rock Hotel, built in the 1860s.

Of local celebrities, I pay a tribute of respect to one who showed me kindness, Mr John Boys, the solicitor, who, good man (a friend of my father's), gave me a position in his office with the kindly intent of making a lawyer of me. The four walls of an office were, however, too limited a sphere for me, and my exuberance of animal spirits, which, as Mr B said, " made a bear garden of the office," rendered it necessary that we should part; but I am glad of the opportunity to pay what is due to his memory. His son, Mr Harvey Boys, I also remember with pleasure and grateful feeling.

I should presume Cranbourne Alley as I recollect it, a sort of *boulevard* of "tagareen shops," or marine stores, stretching from the "Walmer Castle" to Mr Lewis Academy for Young Gentlemen, has in all probability succumbed to the improvement mania, which introduces drainage, ventilation, and health, to the prejudice of the old, quaint, and musty.

Of the medicos of the period – Dr Jarvis, a mighty, pompous, white-headed, gold-capped cane gentlemen, too too utter for ordinary mortals to come near; Dr Waddington (his nephew I believe), a keen, shrew'd practitioner, who understood the Londoner "off the chain" exactly, and administered the corrective colocynth and calomel freely and generally with success; then there was dear old Dr Price, whose bland happy manner rendered physic – however nauseous – pleasant to take if ordered by him. There were other doctors Hoffman, Hunter, and others, but I only knew them by name and remember no peculiarity.

Gloucester Lodge

An old Victorian photograph of Gloucester Lodge, which once stood in Northumberland Road – now Northdown Road – in Margate. Dr Price used the Lodge for his anatomical dissections and research. Opposite Gloucester Lodge was Dr Price's residence, Hoopers Hill House, which was destroyed by enemy fire during WW11.

Margate was then essentially an educational locality. Schools were carried on by John Mickleburgh at Dane Hill House; James Mickleburgh, on the St Peter's road; Stanley, and also Culhill, on the Fort; Newbold, in the Dane (successor to Stanley); and Lewis, at the head of Cranbourne Alley; while for young ladies, there were the Misses Reynolds and Mrs Marinack, and many of the young people who commenced their education in Margate, have in life made their mark and left their "footsteps in the sands of time." I could go indefinitely on as fresh recollections of old, old places and faces well up in the front of memory, and let us hope that the present compares favourably with the past.

I observe that my old townsman and friend[6] in the Colony has left you something respectable to keep his memory green amongst the burgesses of Margate. His kindly generosity and charity is in fair ratio to his wealth, for of his ample store he gives liberally, and there are few old Bendigonians who do not cordially wish him long life and health to enjoy the fruits of his energy and enterprise. Mr Isaac Dyason, his confidential representative in the Colony, is also a Thanet man (Ramsgate), and has made some very favourable mining investments, and "sits warm" according to

---

[6] Viney doesn't mention who he is talking about here but it may have been George Lansell

general belief. Another Margate man, George Adams, is a grand hotel proprietor at Queenscliff, the Margate of the Colony. Mr A. I am happy to say has "guided his gear" to good account, and I believe his property will go into a company, and he will retire from active business. A singular instance of how a word sometimes becomes the key note of an incident. I was a visitor at his hotel years since – on a health recruiting visit to the sea – when walking down with him to meet the steam boat, I remarked that it was "The Husband's Boat[7]." This struck a chord of intelligence, "why you must be a Margate man! So am I," and of course we had many a chat about "St John's Gat."

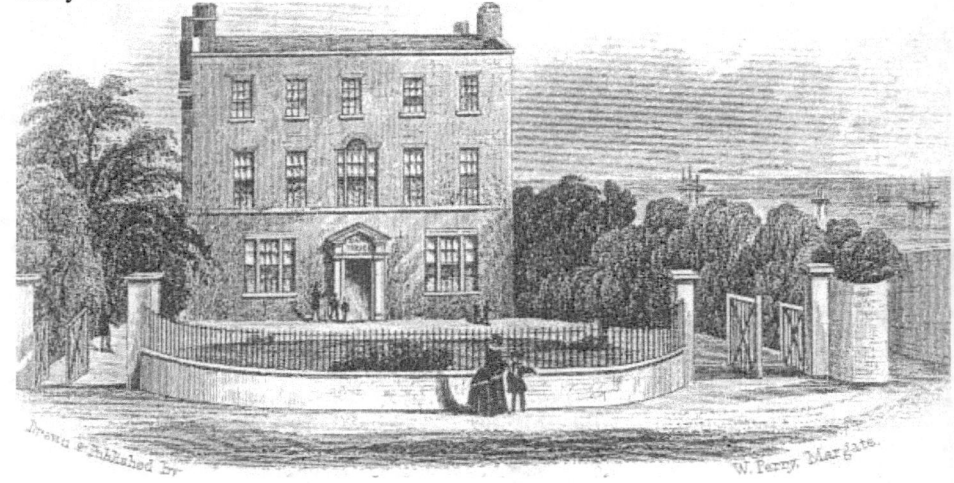

Dane Hill House Academy

During the first half of the 19th century Dane Hill House Academy was one of Margate's best schools for young gentlemen, and was where Viney completed his education under the guidance of Mr John Mickleburgh. It was located in Cliftonville, near the old Pettman's removals depot, somewhere between what is now Athelstan Road and Dalby Square.

I note with much interest the report of your Regatta, it brings to my mind a very early, I think the first, Regatta, about 1828. Of course there was about the same character of boat sailing and rowing competition, a duck hunt, and a blind wheel-barrow race in the harbour at low water – immense fun. Amongst the names of competitors, I note numbers that are memorially familiar, Emptage, Epps, Sandwell, Doughty, Harman, Crump, and others.

Amongst the advertisements I observe that the Staner family have left their old time business at the top of High Street, and gone into the knock-em down business. Mr Levy, J.P., is I apprehend identical with a school fellow of mine at Dane Hill House, then Mrs Mickleburgh's.

---

[7] A boat which left London for Margate each Saturday carrying the fathers of families who lived there during the summer

Margate regatta

Shown here, on an early engraving of one of Margate's Regattas, is the rowing competition of which Viney speaks. Also notice the old sailing ships and early steamboats in the distance.

One of the views gives me the old Reculvers. How well I recollect the old building, it was then a kind of pic-nic place, we usually went by boat, landed and moralised amongst the Golgotha of the old partially washed away churchyard, it has been, I see, necessary to protect the land from the further inroads of the sea by groynes, the old galleries of the church I recollect were of chalk. We used to dine at a small hotel in the neighbourhood, and sailed home in the evening.

My memory brings before me a public, and I think, a free dinner, given *al fresco* on the occasion, I believe, of the passing of the Reform Bill[8], on the piece of ground then fenced in with a high iron railing, and lying and being as a lawyer might say bounded on one side by Upper Marine Terrace, and on another by Lansell's Place or terrace, and on another side by a sea wall, and by the gapway or approach to the sands under the iron bridge. I remember the thing was not deemed a success, the people who partook of it were not educated up to public gratuitous feeds, and misbehaved themselves; rain came on in the afternoon, and my boyish impressions of the scene presented were not edifying, still it was a demonstration, and the country flushed, so to speak with the idea of a splendid and valuable victory obtained, was necessarily a little demonstrative, and that was how Margate got vent on the occasion.

In my former paper I referred to a certain soap boiler's establishment in Bankside. I don't know what name I gave for him, and a rose or a soap boiler would smell as sweet by any other; but the dispenser of odours I referred to was Salter. There was too, I recollect, facing the New Cut, a barber's shop, one Moore, Jemmy Moore I think; the shop, although I did not at that time require much shaving, had its attractions for me, inasmuch as it was a sort of hanging gallery for comicalities and political pasquinades.

---

[8] 1832

Site of the 1832 Reform Bill fiasco

Then there was Mr Faulkner at the corner, a Quaker tailor, who was always shrinking blue pilot cloth on the Fort railings, the true boatmen wear, and I mind memorially that although the fabric was always "shrunk" before being made up, the garments were always built "full and handsome," the trousers turned up a few inches at the bottom, and the coat a size or two too large.

Ghosts, contraband, entertainers, drinks, games

Conjuring up old recollections, I see an old family residence at the end of Cranbourne Alley, opposite what was then Mr Lewis's Academy.

The dwelling presents itself to me as an old Queen Anne house, with two stone steps and pilasters at the sides of the front door; anyway this same domicile had the pleasant reputation of being "haunted." The explanatory legend of how a man therein killed his father, grandmother, or what not, does not remain with me; but I know the boys used to go in bands of half a dozen, towards the evening shades – not by dark, oh no; not if they knew it – to wait expectantly for the appearance of his ghostship, only to scatter and run for dear life when some youth, more imaginative than the rest, would cry out, "there he is! Don't you see it?" I believe the solution of the thing is that some eccentric recluse resides there, and only shewed himself occasionally at the windows.

Cranbourne Alley

This was near the old Six Bells Pub and St John's church. The picture above shows Cranbourne Alley going straight ahead.

Margate boys of that period, I think, had a special *penchant* for ghosts – a relish for the supernatural. There was a traditional ghost too at Albert Square, a little grass plot up behind the Custom House, near Solly's and Gore's boat building shops, but I never saw that spirit. There was some other spots in the neighbourhood where we would not have to venture after dark, and walked quickly through even in daylight; Pump-Lane, and a mysterious alley leading from thence to the Fort, were of this character, and somewhere "down the Dane" was believed to be the very stronghold of the spirits.

Apropos of spirits, there was a very fair stroke of contrabandista carried on in those fine old protection times, anterior to the five Bs – "Bett's British Brandy, Blessed Bad" – or Hodges's cordial, and there was no end of schemes for landing undutied, unexcised liquor over which "the gauger's stick had never passed," and "tubs" or "half-ankers" (small two gallon kegs) were "streamed" and anchored at sea, to be picked up when an opportunity occurred for "running" or landing them. These would be painted a sea-water colour, so as not to attract general attention, the smuggler finding them easily by their bearings; others were painted sand colour, black, or white, as they were to be "planted" on sand, weedy rocks, or chalk, so as not to be noticeable. These were picked up by carters going under the cliff ostensibly to look for sand, seaweed, or chalk; and the blockade, or preventative service man, rigorously examined even a donkey cart, prodding the load with a long iron searcher for kegs of liquor, or packages of tobacco, or other contraband goods. Still cargoes were "run" with impunity.

It has been said, but then the world is censorious, and the tongue of detraction would undo a saint – and it was a damaging rumour against the "Joey" (preventative man) – that he was not proof against a saccharine course of treatment. However, there might not have been any real grounds for the suspicion. A London lady sitting up late at her lodgings on the Marine Terrace was held spell-bound one night to see a boat enter the harbour, cross over to the sea wall, and simultaneously a body of men make their appearance from the roadway leading up to the back of High Street and seize the cargo, and away in a "brace of shakes." Whether it was merely a nightmare, the outcome of an indigestible supper, I know not, and I never heard of any corroboration; but I do remember the seizure of a large galley, 60 feet in length, evidently built expressly for a "run." She was loaded with a large cargo, tubs, &c., in the bottom, and on the thwarts alongside each rower was a bale of tobacco or snuff. The boat had evidently been abandoned by her crew on their finding themselves as it were encompassed by the enemy, the revenue cutter outside and the coastguard-men on the land. She shared the fate of all boats similarly seized, and was sawn into three lengths and sold.

Marine Terrace

These elegant Georgian houses still remain today, though sadly they are no longer fine residences, but house instead thousands of gaming machines, the odd drinking venue, bingo and cafés.

I see by the papers that the old assembly room – the Royal Hotel – has gone by fire[9], as also the block of houses towards High Street. My earliest recollections of "The Royal" are the very successful and then original monologue entertainments

---

[9] The 'Great Fire' of 28 October 1882, described thus: "the last Saturday of October will henceforth become a black letter day in the Margate calendar for at least a century to come"

of the elder Mathews, described as a *conversazione*, and the exhibitions of the peculiar mnemonic powers of the "calculating boy," George Bidder, who eventually became the government calculator, and actuary to a number of grand financial schemes. I must too have seen one of the old fashioned "quality balls," as I have a dim recollection of a scene which I could not have witnessed elsewhere, and as we were friends of the proprietor, Mr C Howe, it is probable I was taken there to see the show.

The Assembly Rooms and Royal Hotel, Cecil Square

The site of the Assembly rooms is now occupied by the Council Offices and the row of Georgian houses to the right is now the site of a bank and Boots the chemist.

Royal Hotel exterior from the other side

I don't suppose Margate, is in reality a more windy place than any other seaport town, but my recollections seem to make it a very "Temple of the Winds" all the winter, and a great deal of the summer, and that in stormy times one had, in order to look seaward, to look round from some corner or point of protection. The sea too, with a strong gale at the top of the springs, was a grand sight and used to play the bear with the Jetty, generally removing a good portion of it. I don't know whether you have the same severe winters, but I remember the Jetty, the portion partially submerged, being covered with ice, and the seaweed also coated with ice and formed into greyish pendants and icicles.

Assembly Rooms interior

This picture represents the kind of scene that Viney recalls when attending "...one of the old fashioned quality balls..." with his family in the 1820s.

I remember an old oddity of that time, one Solly, a poor old man who presented the singular anomaly, while he was hale enough, of always taking a walk to the Jetty head at low water; his mind was so perfectly a blank, that the sight of a young girl lying in the water drowning, having fallen over the Jetty, and the excited appeals of her companion (myself), a mere child, for help, had no effect upon him whatsoever, and the poor girl would doubtlessly have lost her life had not some boatmen, seeing the casualty which had occurred, rushed the boat down, and she was picked up by one Jethro Sandwell – a fine Newfoundland dog, which had got hold of her first, disputing possession. Poor old Solly kept his walk mechanically, and knew nothing of what was passing.

I have known here in Australia two Prebbles, sons of a watchmaker and engraver in Queen Street or Cross Street; also one of the Crofts family, who kept shop near the Market, the Crown, the Lockup, and Tring's, the butcher. But I daresay there are numbers in the Colony from Thanet; only I have not been thrown in juxtaposition with them.

The back of the Bathing Houses

In the background you can see Garner's library with its dome and then, to the right of that, the High Street leading up to the front of the bathing houses. Today, the chalk cliffs below the bathing houses have been incorporated into new shops with split levels and a new road has been built in front forming what is now Marine Drive.

Mr W F Dixon, a prominent mining speculator and musical instrument importer, in Elizabeth Street, is a Margate man, I am told, but I don't happen to know him. There is a Mr Solly, somehow affiliated to the legal profession, son of "Cap'en Solly, of the British System," a little serving mallet of a cutter which used to cart apples over from the Channel Islands. The little vessel's cabin, about 6 ft square, is associated in my young recollection with a delectable tipple for cold weather, called "Dog's nose," which I must have been allowed to taste. I know it was compounded of gin, beer, eggs, butter, sugar and nutmeg. The unnecessary flavouring of coal smoke was imparted to it from careless cookery. I am convinced even at this distance of time, that this same "Dog's nose" was a highly popular concoction, by its gratuitous distribution; and Cap'en Solly was proportionately a man of mark.

Apropos of fashionable drinks of that time, there was the warmed beer of Cobb. Sometimes the warming was affected by the aid of a conical shaped pot, but oftener by being stirred with a red-hot poker up to the required temperature; the former generally imparted a tone of smoke, whilst the latter operation gave it a strong chalybeate or warm flat-irony taste. The poker of the tap-room was generally in demand on cold, outside-comfortless days, at houses which the hoveller [10] frequented, such as the "Hoy" or "Foy Boat."

---

[10] one who assists in saving life and property from a wreck; a coast boatman

Cobb's Brewery. Taken near the Fort

My memory takes me back to my earliest school, somewhere on the Bank, kept by two elderly females of the strictest respectability – decaying gentlewomen they present themselves to me now, in quaint dresses of a still further bygone period – who were compelled by some distressing stroke of fate, to supplement their slender means by a small seminary. I seem to know that they were the relics of a Captain Gunnel, who had distinguished himself, but lost his life by shipwreck, and it is not plain to me now whether whilst commanding a King's ship or the H.E.I.C. ship Hindostan, which was wrecked on Margate sands many years prior to my time.

Boys naturally take that tone of their surroundings and imitate their elders in most things, and the Margate boys of that period – more especially the amphibia, or those who lived on the sea margin – introduced in their play, imitatively, the incidents of the time and the avocations of their fathers. Thus in playing at "Hoop," the toy-circle would be painted with the name of some favourite steamer or popular lugger. And we had our mimic races to London, our more tragic shipwreck or case of distress, carried out, as I recollect it, with more dramatic effect and less palpably absurd anachronism than half the nautical dramas I have sat out in later years. One boy would be placed with his hoop (thrown down), at some point; an ideal spyglass would be put to the eye of some other boy, and it would be announced "a schooner on the Brake!" and away would run the Albion, Fearnought, or what not (hoops, you understand), and tremendous evolutions of boatmanship were performed to get up the standard ship (boy), and much make believe; but very desperate exertions were made to rescue the crew and the Newfoundland dog. Somehow all our stranded ships *had* a dog, a very faithful one of course, who would not leave without the cabin boy in his mouth. Or when we had "worked-up" under the lee of the wreck we hailed in a very Bos'n-ish voice, a sort of *??[11] poitrine* sound, "What ship is that?" "Where are you from?" &c. The distressed youth

---

[11] illegible: 3-4 letters

replied suitably in grievous accents. Then we would sail closer, get alongside, put men on board, run out the anchors, heave her off, and tow her into harbour amid cheers, which made the thing seem almost a reality.

How many of those boys have become men, brave men, and performed these deeds in real life? How many have lost their lives in gallant attempts to do so? Glorious heroes who have gone down ungazetted, and their death comparatively unknown! Possibly the boys of 1883 still keep up the old games, but I am inclined to believe that the more general use of steam has superseded to a large extent the bold avocation of the "Hoveller." Still, when I read your report of the regatta my heart warms with the hope and belief, on seeing the old familiar names that there are still some of the old "do-and-dare" stock left ready to "go off" to the rescue if occasion invited them, justifying the elegiac encomium used in reference to one of the boatmen fraternity, George Philpott, of Deal:

>Full many lives she saved
>With the undaunted crew,
>And put his trust in Providence
>And cared not how it blew.

Tea gardens, Boulevard, donkeys

I don't know whether since I have been, through the columns of the *Gazette, en rapport* with the Isle of Thanet, I have been more observant of anything pertinent to that locality, or whether, not dream't of in our ordinary philosophy, there is some occult mysterious affinity or influence which bring things Thanetical in juxtaposition with me, but I have certainly fallen over just at this period much about the old spot. *Imprimis*, a friend of mine who only has a vague promiscuous idea that I came from "where the hops grow," brought me Ross's book "Margate and Ramsgate, all about and round about them." From its perusal I am refreshed with some pleasant gossip. I find *inter alia* that the Boulevard must have in some course of renovation been repapered, and the earlier glories of Napoleon's Egyptian campaign have given place to the story of Telemachas. Still, I find the staple is still French clocks, pomatum toys, and that sort of thing. One old familiar spot is noticeable by its absence from Mr Ross's book, viz., "St Peter's gardens. Tea gardens by C. Newbolt;" they possibly have been improved off the face of the earth, and the dancing rotunda, and the little alcoves for snug little parties of about two, are gone with them. Well, *sic transit omnia* but there *was* some fun going on there at times. Shallows, I observe, Mr Ross briefly refers to. I am much exercised at a reference to the ruins of Margate abbey in the Grand Hall by the Sea, and my memorial appetite is much whetted to know where it was in early times.

The Boulevard in 1832

If you look carefully at the mural on the right of the Boulevard, you will notice images of pyramids and palm trees, depicting what Viney describes as "...the glories of Napoleon's Egyptian Campaign..."

Ranelagh Tea Gardens in St Peter's

In one of my screeds I described the ceremony of Hoodening in the Isle of Thanet within my memory, and I also referred to the survival of a quaint custom in Wales, "Mary Lloyd," which will be found very generally identical with the accompanying excerpt:

'One of the quaintest customs connected with Christmas still survives in South Wales. It is, perhaps, little more than an unusual form of that method of breaking the silence of the night commonly known as carolling, but instead of going out into the road and singing a greater or fewer number of hymns, more or less out of tune, the Welsh people take unto themselves the skull of a horse. This they adorn with many coloured ribbons, and fasten it upon the head of one of the performers, whose figure is concealed by a sheet. By means of a string attached to the lower jaw of the skull, he claps and rattles the bones, to the real delight and pretended terror of the maid-servants. His companions sing Welsh songs of various kinds, makes a show of restraining the vagaries of the monster, and receive what pence may be bestowed upon them. In some remote parts of "the stormy hills of Wales," the ancient ceremony, of which this mummery is the relic, still lingers. In it the horse's skull and the rest of the paraphernalia are only adjuncts of the custom. The party who thus decorate one of their number strolls from one farmhouse to another, and wherever they call they challenge the inmates to a poetical contest. This is conducted between the insides and the outsides, after the pastoral fashion of Meliboeus and Tityrus, in alternate verses. If, as usually happens, the party of the horse's head succeeded in keeping up verse making longer than the other, they have the right of coming in and being regaled with cakes and ale. If, on the contrary, the farm people manage to perpetrate the last rhyme, the wanderers must go further in search of a supper. No doubt the custom is now giving way to more crowded dwellings and more modern ideas; but it is interesting to come across it now and then, still existing as it has probably done since the time of the Druids.' – *Gentleman's Journal.*

In noticing an early institution of Margate, its donkeys (quadrupedal to prevent misapprehension). I gave a few rhymes from memory, and falling over, in a Melbourne paper, the *ipsissima verba*, I send them along:

At Margate, in the beginning of the present century, a well-known character named Bennett, who let out donkeys on hire, issued the following poetical advertisement, containing a very delicate compliment to his customers:

> Cows' milk and asses too, I sell
> And keep a stud for hire,
> Of donkeys famed for going well,
> And mules that never tire,
> An angel honoured Balaam's ass,
> To meet her in the way,
> But Bennett's troop through Thanet pass
> With angels every day.

I do not recollect Bennett in particular, but I know "the donkey people" as they were generally termed, lived in colonies away "down the Dane," and at the "back of the old church." Time rolls on sure enough if Mr George Watson is or rather has been forty years her Majesty's Postmaster. I look back through a vista of his predecessors Mannings, Gore, and Valder, the office then being in the lower High Street, opposite "the bathing rooms."

Donkey people

I think I have in former notices referred to some Margate men who are men of mark here, George Lansell, George Adams, and others, and I may add another, Solly, a grandson of old Cap'en Solly, who fifty years ago or more used to sail a little cutter, "The British System," and traded between the Channel Islands, or Flanders and Margate. This young man has so improved his opportunities as to attain the position of Senior Usher at the Scotch College, one of our best public schools. His father, at one time in Mr Boys's office, still keeps up a connection with the legal profession of Melbourne.

A very grand marriage came to occur quite lately, in which a descendant of a Margate resident played a prominent part – the bride! Mr Cooper, M. L. A. (Queensland), and Barrister, married a daughter of Mr JB Watson, a quartz millionaire, or more comprehensively, a lucky digger, Mrs Watson having been the daughter of a rope maker near the Jolly Sailor. The wedding was of a most gorgeous character, and the catalogue of the bride's trousseau occupied a couple of columns of the local paper.

Children's games, chalk, packets & steamships, art

Reading over your pleasant *multum in parvo* "Guide to Margate," which by your kindness came to hand this mail, some few other memories of the past are revived, and which you will, on your editorial discretion, use or consign to the tophet of troublesome communications – the waste paper basket.

We are a great people here for fire brigading, which starting from a few volunteer companies in the provinces of Bendigo (Sandhurst), the first in 1855, of which I had the honour to be an active member and officer for several years, the institution has expanded itself, in fact "taken root." Its annual gatherings and keen competitions are events only exceeded in interested by our racing carnival, "The Cup" week; and the very little boys in the street imitate the action of the brigades in their practice, by running a little child's perambulator, or something of that kind, down the street, to represent a mimic fire engine or hose reel, an illustration of how the childish mind is tinctured by the scene amid which the child lives and has its being.

The above, by way of preamble to a remembrance of a boyish amusement of the youngsters living down towards the Margate Harbour, and more especially associated with the boatmen, those who

> When in the storm on Albion's coast,
> Dare the dangerous wave,
> And go the crew to save.

In the cold severe winter weather, when any game which did not involve physical exertion and sequentially warmth of body would not have been popular, the trundling of hoops was the favourite amusement for the winter evenings when "the stormy winds did blow;" and with a natural association our hoops were named and made to represent the various steamboats running between London and Margate. We did competitive "spins," or (what was, I think, the more popular form), each assumed the character of one of the well-known luggers of the period. The area lying between the Jetty end, Bankside, The White Hart, and the slipway and Little Beach was ideally mapped out as the North Sea with its sands. One boy had to accept the *rôle* of "a ship on shore" on such and such a sand, and after a little simulated dramatic action of a man on the look-out, a report of "a ship on shore," minute guns, &c., off went the lugger "Victory," the "Albion," the "Friendship," or what not, to her assistance, and the difficulties and hazardous character of the service were, as I recollect, rendered with an attention to details which would put to shame by comparison many a representation of this kind of thing in our theatres. Of course there were unheard of difficulties in beating up to the stranded ship, superhuman exertions in getting out anchors, heaving her off, keeping her afloat, and towing her into harbour. At other times we saw signals of distress flying somewhere away by the first lamp post on the parade wall, and away helter skelter went a fleet of luggers (hoops) in the heaviest of weather, shipping tremendous seas all the way, and the first aboard getting the "hovel" to bring off an anchor of fabulous weight and chain to match, and as I remember it, all this was gone through with a gravity and affected reality which made it quite exciting. In the matter of an anchor being required, there was no hitch in our "make-believe." We had Mr Cobb's office, where we got an order for the required anchor, &c., and the whole thing was gone through in its entirety. How few, probably, of that little crowd continue to trundle the hoops of real life!

We have here, I find, some other scions of Margate houses, *inter alia* a Prebble, a watchmaker's son, who follows the business in Kyneton; also one of the Crofts, who in my time occupied premises near the lock-up and Bartlett's Crown and Cushion, or something of that sort. Going through the advertisements of *Keble's Gazette*, which I do most religiously, I note some old familiar names, whilst many others, well remembered, appear conspicuous by their absence – joined the majority, I suppose.

It is not often that the advent of a social entity, a mere "commoner," is flashed round the world by electric agency. Your townsman, Mr George Lansell, however, having been presented by a son and heir, the wires told his friends – and there is a good lot of them – that each was the case within twenty-four hours of the event coming off. And I am given to understand that a bottle or two were cracked on old Bendigo on receipt of the news.

To you of the Isle of Thanet, who, as it were live and have your being amongst chalk, it will be strange, but it is an actual geological fact, that this Continent knows it not, and that the only chalk we know of is imported; and therefore a sight of the white cliffs of old England would be welcome as a novelty, apart from other and more endearing associations. We have it in its higher crystallised form of marble truly, but not as the old familiar chalk, and it is by no means an easy task to convey to the minds of those who have not seen those masses of deposits, how it can be cut out, more especially as proposed in the trans-channel tunnel from Dover.

Passenger boats, cross-channel trade, paintings

It is open to grave doubt whether your readers feel the pleasure in reading that I do in writing of the events of half a century gone by. Should you, Mr Editor, think, as the French say, the game is worth the candle, by all means put them in print; if, on the contrary, consign them to the limbo of the waste paper basket.

My mind goes back then to the time, as chronological datum, before the building of the present lighthouse on the pier, and, by a natural association to the local shipping of the period and the trade of the port. Some of the early humorists and song-wrights, or writers, have immortalised "The Margate Hoy," in descriptions of the incidental fun and discomforts of the early voyagers from Cockaigne to the abode of Hygeia, the Isle of Thanet. I have before me mentally the last remnant of that "line of packets" which were run off the roads (Margate Roads) by the advent of the steamboat. I see a stout-built round-sterned obese kind of ark, with carved rudder head and ancient tiller, the White Horse and "Invicta" prominent thereon. This is the Hoy[12] "Thanet," of which Captain Malpas, a portly weather-beaten man, is present commander; she once brought down the *élite* of Margate's visitors, now she is a mere carrier of goods and merchandise. Coeval with the "Thanet," I see a smarter class of sloop, "The Countess of Elgin," sailed by John Stranach, one of a long family of Margate mariners; "The Lord Hawkesbury," Mr Blain master; "The Fox," owned and sailed by the Fox family.

These crafts for some years connected the coast of Flanders and England, carting over horses, butter, cheese, eggs, rabbit, walnuts, fowls, &c., while a smaller craft, "The British System," made bolder stretches, under the command of one Solly, to the Channel Islands, and returned with apples in bulk. I don't think there was a boy in St John's Parish but was fully acquainted with the little sloop and her arrival, and for a few days after her making fast to the pier there was a very "carnival" in

---

[12] flat-bottomed barge

the direction of specked apples; explanatorily, "specked" apples were those bruised or damaged in the passage, and sold at reduced rates. Youth is accredited with a cast-iron stomach, and all the "specked" fruit went off rapidly. Later on, I may say interpolatively, it was my privilege to lie in the Hooghly (Calcutta), near a smart little barque, bearing the name of a well-known brewer, Thomas Spence, from memory (he had a brewery in the Dane), and hailing from Margate.

Steam packet arriving in Margate

Going back to the earlier date, when steam began to assert itself as a marine motor, I see, *inter alia*, the Albion, Dart, Magnet, Harlequin, and Columbine, podgy little vessels with overgrown paddle-boxes and very little comfort. They gradually gave place to a better class of packets, Royal George, William, and Adelaide; these, again, were beaten off by improved craft, Red Rover, Herne, and others; and, looking at your present services, no doubt smart screw-propellers with every improvement and convenience that an advanced civilization has induced, the comparison is a pleasant one. Still there was much fun – always provided it was fine weather – in voyaging from the Custom House Wharf to Margate Pier or Jetty; and what, between liquid refreshments, mild flirtations, and an untiring "band" – *that* harp, *that* cornopean[13], and "the same fiddle" – the seven or eight hours voyage was worried through agreeably enough.

For a time a regular passenger service by steam was maintained between Margate and the Netherlands by the steamboat "Enderneming," Captain Cowham, and for a period the mails from the continent were brought to Margate by two steamboats, respectively "The Fury" and "The Spit-fire," but eventually influence shifted the route to Dover.

---

[13] keyed bugle

The Harlequin at Margate Pier

Apropos of the sailing traders to the Netherlands, there was a considerable flood of art, resultant in the production by a Dutch sailor – Nepos, by name – of "false presentments" of the several vessels above-named. These hardly came strictly within the canons of true art; were, perhaps, somewhat wanting in perspective, and – well, we had not then seen Higgins's and other artists in marine subjects, and with a big burgee[14] flying the name of the ship, and a detailed legend at foot further telling you it was intended for the Countess of Elgin, Ostend, bearing S.E. by E. 1/3 E., and a windmill in the distance to help the imagination. He must be a carping critic who would find fault with minor details. Perhaps some of these triumphs of pictorial art are still extant. I would walk a few miles to renew my acquaintance with them.

S. W. Viney   Melbourne, Australia

---

[14] square swallow-tailed flag

Responses to Viney's Recollections

The "Hooden Horse"

Early 20th century Hoodeners with their Horse

Sir, – perhaps you will allow me to state that the Hooden horse is *not* an extinct animal, but that he was in full vigour at Monkton on Christmas Eve. He may probably survive another Christmas and visit Margate, or he might, if it would interest your visitors, be on the sands when the season is on.

Mr Viney is not quite correct in describing the manners and objects of all Hooden horse troupes. As I, and others in Thanet were, in our younger days, in the fun, perhaps you will permit me to describe our troupe. Our party consisted of six. About six weeks before Christmas we began our practice nights for learning carols, and, as most of us belonged to the old village choir, when a fiddle, clarionet, flute, and bassoon formed the church music, we endeavoured to sing in tune and time, and judging by the *black-mail* collected, and spent well, our words were understood.

The first in attraction was the "horse," a piece of wood formed into a horse's head; the lower jaw was on hinges, and when out of temper his champing was terrific; to this lower jaw a string was attached, under the control of the lad covered over with sacking. Into the head of the "horse" was fixed a stake, so high that the lad under the sack, when bent, gave a fair representation of a horse. On the "horse" was the "jockey," another lad with a well-stuffed gaberdine, so that a fall would not hurt him. Then there was "Molly" a lad dressed in woman's clothes with her broom. When our carol was done and the door of the house we were at, opened, the "horse" began to kick, and in went "jockey," if possible into the door, "Molly" at the same time using her broom energetically, and all trying to make a bit of fun.

One of our party carried a bag which was well filled with apples from the farm houses before we arrived home, which were consumed during Christmas.

This was our *rural* way of Hoodening, perhaps the custom became degenerated in your town, and the followers of "Hoden" would not take the trouble of learning to sing, like too many waits of the present day; and the same applies to hand-bell ringing. A cracked horse-bell is considered good enough to gather together a few pence, and any noise to pass for singing; but these are counterfeits and not sterling Hoodeners of the days gone by.

Yours truly, R. B.   Minster, Thanet

"Ye Haunted House"

A Legend, by C. M.

The following has reference to the haunted house referred to by Mr Viney in his "Recollections of Margate:"-

Have you ever seen a house whose walls are crumbling to the ground here, green with damp and mildew there, whose very windows are warped and screwed into shapes that of themselves would frighten you-a house whose whole appearance suggests a fit abode for one "not of this world?" If you have, shut your eyes to it now-this house is of a different stamp. Oh, yes a plain, unpretentious brick building; it has been described as of the "Queen Anne style," but be that as it may, it is so minus of anything like architectural beauty that it would be cruel indeed to attach to it any particular data or style.

Many years ago the inmates (for this house was occupied-in more senses than one!) were invariably awoke in the dead of the night by a current of cold air similar to that caused by shaking a sheet or blanket in a room; the repeated occurrences of this led eventually to a "watch" being arranged, and, lo! "at the witching hour of night" a form in shape and movement similar to a human being (the lower portion, however, being lost in its vapour-like draperies) appeared, surveyed the premises, taking particular notice of the "watchers," and then – in common with ghosts – disappeared or melted into air.

The house at that time boasted the name of "Angel House," and this was boldly inscribed on a tablet of stone built in at the corner of the house, and the impression prevailed that the term "Angel" had caused displeasure, and that a devil had been sent to dwell there. The word was therefore stopped up and that of "Angle" painted over it (albeit a more appropriate name, the house standing on a triangular piece of ground). This, however, did not have the desired effect, for from a room that had a partition, the top of which is glass to lend light to other compartments (I cannot vouch for this never having been in the house), the form was constantly seen to glide past and enter the room.

A few years since the roof was completely lifted out of its place and bid fair to fall to the ground in front of the house, and the ghost never having been seen since this occurrence it is conjectured that it took its departure via the roof, shunning the front and back doors which were mortal's means of exit. N.B. The ghost was generally believed to be of the feminine gender.

Jottings From Australia

Dealing with lazy *émigrés*, Ly-ee-moon shipwreck

By a Native of Margate

Topics of general interest to your readers are few out here; still there is one in which a large number are interested, and which may convey a useful lesson as to why many who have come out here to throw in their lot with us are dissatisfied with the result. They come expecting too much; immediately on starting for the new world they seem to think the original curse as it is called – I think it is one of the blessings to work when one is fairly remunerated for one's labour – is suspended, and on landing they kick up their heels, play up high jinks, and generally put on thrills. This lasts for a time, but in the end it generally disgusts the best friends of such persons. In illustration of this, I may say that a friend of mine gives me the narrative of an *émigré* from your own locality.

My friend writing to a local paper said he would gladly give advice, the result of many years experience, to anyone coming to Australia, and in response he received a letter from a perfect stranger who wished to emigrate. My friend furnished the advice asked for, and by return he received the announcement "he and wife had sailed on such a date," with the request that my friend would procure a house or lodgings for them, and work for the man. In the uncertainty as to the ship's arrival, being a sailing vessel, to carry out the first part of the request would have been a manifest absurdity; and as to the second part one could hardly be expected to find work suitable for a person whom one had never seen or knew anything about. However, to meet the difficulty, my friend forwarded a letter through the ship's agents to be handed to the man on his arrival, directing him to go to a certain highly respectable and reasonable economic Temperance Hotel (as the applicant described himself as a blue ribbon man).

My friend further went to the hotel and made the best arrangements for the reception of his correspondent. After some term of expectancy the new arrival presented himself in anything but a propitiatory condition and in utter disregard of the axiom about first appearances and a confounded habit of "Yes-zurring" and forelock-pulling at every other word. Where was he staying? "At a hotel" of not too bright a reputation as a residence. What could he do? What had he been doing? "Well" (with much more "zurring" and capping) "farming work and that." My friend on going home consulted with one of the clearest headed women on any of the continents. "What are we to do with them?" "Why, get them a house, and get them into it *at once*. I saw one today in ——— Street, which would suit. Here, stay till I get my bonnet on, &c.," and in half an hour we had a house hired, a week's rent paid, and I on my way to the new arrivals with the key.

With a little energy these people were domesticated the next day. Then about work? My friend "laid" the new comer on to it at once, and in spite of his very yokel and indolent habit kept him there for some time, but it was "werry hard work." With a vigorous turn of mind and a belief that almost anyone makes a better master for himself than any other man, my friend suggested to this whilom clod compeller that it would be well to try and knock up a business on his own account, and as he was not a mechanic or tradesman it was suggested that amongst the various odd jobs, such as carpentering, painting, and gardening, carpet-beating, cleaning, and planning should be included. Some cards were feebly got out, and may be distributed within a certain radius, as it had been proposed, with a view to working up a little connection.

But the carpet business was objected to, and from lack of anything like energy, or that admirable faculty of "waiting," nothing came of the plan; the party abandoned the idea of making himself independent and went to work as an engineer's labourer, beyond which, even if he had any mechanical genius or ability, the jealousy of the duly trained apprenticed artisan will in all time prevent him from obtaining admittance into the craft.

With this I have nothing to complain, but my friend further informs me that it has come to his knowledge that some indignation has been expressed at the idea of his suggesting that they "should come ten thousand miles to shaike car-pits." Here, we do not think anything honest to be unworthy of performance, and it is a singular corollary to the vulgar outburst above to state that a man, coming from within a mile or two of this same person's home, has, with even less educational advantages, actually built up a business on this very carpet cleaning, and so improved himself educationally and financially that he became an excellent and capable contributor to a science journal on conchology and fossils, and left his wife and family with a really good remunerative business, dying, all to soon, a very worthy self-made man. So much for "shaikin' car-pits" in Victoria.

We have just experienced a sad shock in the wreck of the steamer Ly-ee-moon, a steamer of some 750 tons, which struck on Green Cape, on the east coast of North Holland, and went down with some 70 passengers and crew, only 15 being left to tell the story of their miraculous escape. It is the old coasting casualty story, hugging the land in foggy weather, and shaving the jutting point to save half a mile in the journey. This should be a lesson, and teach the travelling public that in this continued encouragement of goading of captains to make quick passage – to save a quarter of an hour in a three days' voyage – They are really contributing to these frightful, but preventable, catastrophes.

Our obituary notices will not probably be highly interesting to you, but in the case of the one I send there may be some still living who would have known him: – "Capp – At his residence, Fyans-street, Chilwell, Geelong, Robert F. Capp, aged 91 years, formerly farmer, of Sholden, near Deal, Kent, England."

I noticed in one of your papers the other day an advertisement inviting parents to send their daughters to a school at Ramsgate, referring to "the well-known salubrity of the Isle of Thanet," and fate and circumstances a few days since threw me into juxta-position with a whilom Margate school boy, Mr M. Nasmyth, new architectural engineer in the mines.

Another old time Margatian, Mr J Philpott, many years here and Sydney, left some time since to enjoy the *Otium cum dig.* of many years successful trading; he resides now at Tunbridge Wells.

Charity performances, showmen, carnival, New Guinea, lost wreck

By a Native of Margate

Trollope gave as one of the outcomes of his visit to us Australians that we were given to "blowing" – English exaggerating ourselves – "blowing our own trumpet." Well, possibly he was right, but at the risk of further verifying his estimate of us, I cannot help giving you a little story which I think is creditable to us in consideration of the object which incepted it.

"In faith and hope the world will disagree,
But all mankind's concerned in charity."

And so it came about that one of our Asyla for the relief of those "distressed in mind, body, or estate," a material hospital wanted an extension, a new wing, and Miss Genevieve Ward, the actress – only a strolling player, mind – conceived the idea of a special play or recital for the purpose. Sophocles's great tragedy "Antigone" was selected. The matter was taken up; fashionable seats were secured at fabulous prices, and, in brief, a sum of £2,681 was the result towards the £5,000 required.

Clarence Whistler, a wonderful athlete or wrestler, has just finished his career, advisedly dying from the result of dissipation. With a great record as an exponent of the potentialities of nature from America he, like Caesar, might have said he came, saw, and conquered all opponents – but himself got on the drink – stated at 30 (thirty) bottles of champagne a day (say half, or further allowing for newspaper exaggeration, a quarter); gave himself away to foolish reckless feats of strength and imprudence *inter alia*, masticating and swallowing glasses, with a very natural result, breakdown, inflammation, collapse, and death. It is painful to recollect how many men of the showmen class; more or less gifted physically or mentally, have gathered the laurel here only to overlay it with the cypress.

Our "Cup-day," which really means a week's Saturnalia amongst all classes – a gathering from the circumjacent colonies who flock to the centre city, Melbourne, "to see the Cup run." For weeks previous to the event the dressmaking sisterhood are working their fingers off and the *providores* of various kinds are busy beyond description in the laying in of commissariat stores for the expected heat. A few days before the various railways shoot down the crowds, the steamboats from the various colonies disembark their thousands, and the caterers for public accommodation are driven to their wit's end where to put the arrivals. Baths are improvised into beds, and even our billiards tables have to do duty as four-posters. The theatres and other places of amusement fill – well, that's no name for it – sardine is better – and the whole place is given over to festivity – in some places pandemonium.

The end of the week is the end of the carnival, and the visitors toil back to their respective homes perhaps wiser, with improved experiences, if not better men and women, for what between the lay and professional magsmen[15], the betting men, and other sharp practitioners, they generally leave with a new "wrinkle" or two, although the course of learning may have been more or less expensive.

---

[15] confidence tricksters

Thus October 7 concludes the series of "Cup" jollities, and after a brief recess the "New Year meetings," with more horse racing, betting, and all-round dissipation, commences, and we are gorged with another week or fortnight of pleasure; of course, not having been in Rome when *Circenses et panem* was the popular cry, I can't say how far we assimilate to those ardent lovers of "Scenes in the Circle," but historically there is some parallel, and – where is Rome now?

Our first organised attempt to really prospect New Guinea has, it is to be regretted, has turned out badly and news rather meagre has been received telling of the massacre of the whole party (13) on the Fly River. The expedition was very well equipped either for conciliatory, defensive, or offensive action towards the natives, and in the absence of further intelligence we are at a loss to know how the thing came about. From personal experience (nearly forty years since), I am aware that the natives are acquisitive, bold, and combative, and it is probable that the chance of a loot of the equipment has led to the sad result, and I suppose if it is ordained that we – a superior race – are to occupy and enjoy this valuable island, it must be by the usual method – improving the aborigines off the face of the earth, or at any rate reducing them to an inconsiderable minimum. I have referred to this island (New Guinea) as a "valuable" one, because I am satisfied that I saw some of the natives decorated, together with shell and other matters, with pieces of gold, and to this superadded its tropical and insular character, it is bound to become sooner or later one of the fortuitous outvents for the surplus population of the more overcrowded parts, and open up further markets for the productions of the manufacturer. The resources, mineral, botanical, and animal of New Guinea, are numerous and varied.

There is an old joke about a man buying a piece of land only to find that "another fellow has got his land on the top of it." And whether this ever occurred in relation to real property there is no direct evidence, but a somewhat analogous case comes to occur in the matter of the wreck of the fine steamer, the Gulf of Carpentaria, which took a short-cut in the bank's Straits, touched on an unknown rock, and sunk. The wreck was sold by the underwriters to a Mr Marsh for £200, and now the purchaser can't find his property, and is offering £100 to anyone who will find it and put a buoy on it. Looking for a wreck in fifteen fathoms of water, position unknown, is like looking for the proverbial needle in the bundle of hay.

A Chapter About Dogs

(*Cave Canem*, old school song)
By a Native of Margate

Starting out with the distinct assertion that no one better "loves to hear the honest watchdog's bark, "no one has a higher appreciation of the well-known fidelity of the canine race, nor has a higher recognition of the wondrous sagacity verging on intelligence in that excellent companion of man – one, by-the-bye, that never argues, "answers back," or "nags" him – I am compelled by an inward consciousness to admit that no animal goes or has gone further – unintentionally and innocently, no doubt – to verify Paul's sweeping assertion that "all men are liars" than our four-footed friend. Men can talk and write on almost any other subjects in a precise methodical matter-of-fact style, and with a generally due regard to strict veracity they can put a certain amount of gloss on any other non-canine narrative and just keep within the four corners of credibility, perhaps as the Empress Eugenie once said of General Trochu, "just skirting the truth," but just keeping out of the broad sweep of the Apostle's assertion. But just take the chain off and let the favourite dog – if dead so much the better – loose, and in a few minutes the narrator will be up to eyebrows of startling Munchausenisms about *that* dog, and the listener's hair will lift his hat off at the bold assertions of utterly impossible events in connection with that dog, the extravagance of one story being out-Heroded by another which only serves to put another hearer "in mind" of an incident, &c., till in self defence an average truthful man has to scare up something about *his* dog or dogs, however divergent from actual fact.

This may seem a harsh condemnation, but as proof let my readers test the matter when on a journey with promiscuous co-travellers. Just start a mild dog story of a really truthful and sequentially tame character. Let him then notice how No. 2 will launch a tale, dog and all, with a little spice of romance about it. No. 3 will then give you one "which one would hardly believe if he had not seen it himself." No. 4 will furnish an extreme improbability – an impossibility but that he vouches for its truth. Not to be outdone, the next will go bald-headed into a most reckless demonstration of utter impossible quantities as far as canine ethics are concerned, and unless the experimenter wishes to be thoroughly impressed with Paul's doctrine he had better clear at this stage.

This peculiarity is not novel. In almost all historic times the dog has been made the vehicle for an indulgence in that easily besetting sin so brusquely denounced by the early father. The writer of the Odyssey insists upon Ulysses being recognised and welcomed – after his twenty years' absence – by his faithful "dawg," but even had the animal (the dog, I mean) been in his blind puppyhood when the great warrior left, twenty years is far and away beyond the average span of a dog life, and I therefore fear that Homer, who sometimes nodded, had herein skirted the truth.

History, sacred and profane alike, points to the dog as an early companion to man, and I have little doubt the popular infirmity of "making the most of him" has existed in all time, and he has been as now traditionally made the subject of many little fictions, which have become *facts* from repeated reiteration. However, many a human history and especially autobiographical sketches would bear some judicious paring down to fit square into truth; therefore as kindly remembrance of a generally attached and disinterested follower, man may be allowed to give glowing pictures of his favourite's virtues.

The above is written *apropos* of a composition in the *Standard* (London) headed "Intelligent dogs," the writer of which goes in bald-headed to an assertion that a certain dog, hungry or otherwise, would not eat biscuit offered in the name of Mr Gladstone, but would joyfully accept it if told it was from "the Queen" – an ultra loyal dog, who would "lie down and die for the Queen," would give "three cheers for the Queen" (three barks) to order, &c. Surely this writer had never seen "the learned pig," or the many show dogs, who do all sorts of things by a careful training in the observances of the intonation or manner of the master. We have a dog here at Port Melbourne who sees every train off and marches or "runs in" any slack-in-stays passengers, and when he sees the porter about to ring the starting bell he anticipates him by a loud bark, and so really "starts the train," but, of course, he has been *trained* to do this, and there is no "intelligence" in it whatsoever.

The Goodwins

These same sands have now for some centuries been well known and the comparatively smooth water anchorage or roadstead, which their protection forms, is world famous in history and song. Here Caesar (anterior to the Goodwins), landed his legions; some local historians go the length of pointing at the identical spot where the standard bearer of the Tenth Legion leaped down, and as some one says "re-animated the instincts of discipline." Here Dibden lays the *locale* of one of the grandest of dramas "Black-eyed Susan" (although by the way my reminiscence of the Deal girl does not go in the direction of that particular eye) and "All in the Downs," and Russell has immortalised "The Boatmen of the Downs" just as Barham (Ingoldsby) has made a memory of "The Foy," "Cobb's XX, " and "Jarvis's Landing Place;" therefore possibly a "screed" on the subject may have its interest for some of your readers.

Probably no locality in the wide world is so well known as these same dangers of the sea, whether it be in their more serious character as the great "ship swallowers," the grave of thousands; or in their lighter aspect as an illustration of a *non quitur* in the adage "as much to do with it as Tenterden steeple has with the Goodwin Sands," which rose as we learn from a piece of quaint old history that in the reign of Henry VIII, somewhere early in the 16th century. Attention being drawn to this "*shelfe* of sand" as it was called, that stopped up Sandwich Haven, and Lord Chancellor Moore coming down as a Commissioner to enquire of "such as were thought to be men of experience and men that could of likelihood best certify him of that matter," amongst others came an "old grey-headed man that was thought to be little less than a hundred years old." To him spake the Chancellor, "Father tell me what is the cause of this great rising of the sands and shelves here about this haven of Sandwich? Ye are the oldest man that I can espy in this assembly, so that if any man can tell any cause of it ye of likelihood can say most of it." "Yea, forsooth good Master Moore," quoth this old man, "for I am well nigh a hundred years old, and no man here present is near unto my age." "Well then," quoth the Chancellor, "how say you in this matter?" "Sir," quoth he in reply, "I am an old man, I think that *Tenterden Steeple* is the cause of Goodwin Sands, for I am an old man Sir, and may be, I remembering the building of Tenterden steeple, and I may remember when there was no steeple at all, and before that Tenterden steeple was in building there was no speaking of flats or sands that stopped the haven and therefore I think that Tenterden steeple is the cause of Goodwin Sands and of the destroying and decay of Sandwich Haven." I have heard of a feeble attempt to establish something like rationality in the old man's reply, by an endeavour to establish an hypothesis that the revenues which should have been expended in engineering works, groins, &c., to maintain the channel were diverted for the building of Tenterden steeple. This argument, however, must

> ".............fall like an inverted cone
> Wanting a proper base to stand upon,"

– and we must look for something more reasonable.

It is pretty evident from the above enquiry that the decay of the Sandwich Haven and the appearance of the Goodwins were simultaneously or contemporaneous events, and we must, in seeking for a solution of the matter, not look upon the "Sandwich Haven" there spoken of as in its present condition a mere pea-soupy little river, but to have been a wide estuary or tidal way open probably right through what are now the Minster Levels (marshes) into the embouchure of the Thames at Reculvers (the Regulbium of the Roman period), and which in Juvenal's time must have been a deep water course between the Isle of Thanet and the mainland of Kent, as he refers to the Richborough shore as "deep." *"Rutupinove edita fundo ashea callebat,"* and there is a little doubt from other classic passages that this was the route taken to reach "Augusta" (London) by the Romans, thus avoiding the rounding of the stormy Foreland. Accepting these premises as granted we cast about for some tangible causation for the closing of this race or passage, and thanks to the possession of one of the Ordnance maps of that part of Kent (kindly sent me by a dear old East Kent friend, Geo. F. Fry, one of the Dover Aldermen) and the use of a chart of the North Sea and English Channel (as kindly placed at my disposal by another dear old Kentish friend, Captain H. Cooper Keen, of the ship "Darling Darns") I am able to offer an hypothesis which seems to me to "hold water." That the sea level on the north coast of Kent has been at some period materially higher, will be clear to anyone who will notice the geological formation of Margate at the time when the fleets of Caesar passed through from Richborough past Reculvers *en route* to the Thames. The sea doubtlessly extended all through the valley (the "Brooks" in my early time) which lies between the south end of Margate and Tivoli, and also up the Dane, in fact, tidally covered all the low lying ground, and "St John's at Meergate" only existed on the cliff and high grounds, and thus there would be a strong and deep "race" through the Minster valley where now filled up with alluvial deposit, the rationale of its filling up being, that, from causes which I shall attempt to explain hereafter, the water finding an easier outlet in another direction, no longer rushed through there, gravitation of course commences, and what was once a rapid estuary became what it is now – green pastures.

All or many residents will be aware that the Foreness which stands between Margate and the North Foreland, is a point standing boldly out to the north; many who are connected with the water will be aware that a "spit" or under water rock runs out perhaps two miles further even than the Ness itself,[16] and assuming that in the days anterior to the Goodwin Sands this was a lofty headland standing out still further, it will to the experienced or observant not be difficult to realise the natural result that an immense volume of water would be "penned" or "held up" in the bay which such headland would then form, and the collected tidal waters of the North

---

[16] The chart shows that the point shoals a long distance out four or five miles from the actual cliff, and the soundings clearly indicate the continuance of a ridge of rock seaward in almost a direct line for the "Knock" or "Galloper," both of which obstacles have no doubt a basis of chalk, although covered with sand. – S.W.V.

Sea, Thames, and Medway would rush through the readiest opening (the present Minster Valley), and, assuming that some great convulsion of nature – some tidal wave or severe gale – swept away the extended promontory (Ness, nez or nose), the tides would then sweep round the Foreland, the direction of the force being diverted over towards the French coast, and the natural eddies bringing in and depositing sand on the ridge of rock (chalk probably) which forms the basis of the Goodwin, and accumulation would in a short time present itself in a ridge, or ridges, of sand. Of course, this is but a speculation, but I conceive that I have made out a tolerably good case – a reasonable solution of the much vexed question of "the origin of the Goodwin," and certainly one with as much claim to probability and credibility as that submitted by our old friend to "Master Moore."

As a further argument in favour of the belief that less facility was offered – in the period before the Goodwins and Shelfes – for the escape of the waters from the North Sea, we may observe that the Essex marshes and many parts of the eastern seaboard of England were more or less under water, and have since been reclaimed from the sea and utilised. Hazarding a conjecture, it is not too much to conceive the passage from the Downs into the North Sea, by way of the Foreland, to have been but a comparatively narrow channel in regard to the vast amount of water which tidal equalization sent up and down; probably a rapid and dangerous race similar to that round the Bill of Portland and many other places where large volumes of water have to change position, as tides, in short spaces of time. Hence the probability that the short cut by way of Sandwich, Richborough, and Reculvers was the more popular route.

That some great changes has taken place at some period is apparent by the changes of the average water level, and that places once evidently submerged (tidally) are silted up and no longer overflowed, as instance the Minster Levels, the Brooks and the Dane at Margate, Seasalter, Graveney, and many other localities on the northern shores of Kent.

I do not know that any very important practical moral may be deduced from the determination of this question beyond the showing how the alteration of one portion of our physical geography may produce remarkable effects at another part, and while we congratulate ourselves on the triumphant success of man's engineering ability it may be well to previously count the possible cost in some unexpected rising up of "shelfes and sand," the development of some obstacles to navigation, or the partial submergence or flooding of country previously habitable and productive. To anyone who may take an interest in this subject I would recommend an inspection of the Ordnance Map (geological) of Kent, which, I have no doubt, would go largely in the direction of making him a convert, to some extent, of my views.

It may possibly be contended that there has been a general diminution of the waters of the North Sea; but it will be observed that the reduction in the mean of the water level – that is the retirement of the sea from low lying ground – has been comparatively *local*, the S.E. coast of Essex and Suffolk, the N.E. portion of Kent, and the Dutch coast lying over against it.

Assuming my speculations to have any force, then, looking back through a vista of years, we may idealise old Margate, standing on a point of high land contained between the Dane and the "Brooks," or valley, which came in through where the Lower Marine Terrace and new sea wall are now built; in fact, on the ridge which represents High Street, Cecil and Hawley Squares, &c., the presence of the church in that locality, and the absence of old buildings on the north side of the Dane, give some show of confirmation to the idea, and there is equally as little doubt that the Dane, then a creek or arm of the sea running up to Hartsdown, formed a natural harbour for the rude boats of the hardy islanders of that time; and, following up this train of thought on the spot, no doubt much interesting speculation might be indulged in – all more or less feasible and probable – of the life and times of the early residents of St John's at Meregatt.

It is not too much to believe that the rocks (chalk) now tidally submerged mark the outline of the lofty cliffs of bygone days, which have gradually succumbed to the influences of weather and the beating surge, and if so, we may in our mind's eye, looking back a handful of centuries, when historic time was young, see beetling cliffs projecting out nearly as far as the Pier now extends on the one hand, meeting a bold headland (its site now indicated by the Nayland) coming from the western side forming a narrow entrance into a convenient little natural harbour for the tempest tossed mariner and his frail vessel.

Broadstairs is another instance of a natural harbour, and must have been popular to some extent, as we find that "our ladie of Bradstard" had a chapel there: *notabilium*. Our ancient mariners were of a pious turn of mind or very superstitious and wherever was a harbour there was also a "chapel," a sort of moral Droit-office, where the mariner escaped from impending wreck might perform his devotions and gratefully offer his oblations. Ramsgate is an artificially constructed harbour, and could not have been known in the age to which this little paper refers, Sandwich, Stonar, and Richborough being the only ports on the south side of Thanet, or that part of Kent.

I apprehend this subject is of sufficient importance in an archaeological sense to awaken an interest amongst your readers and give rise to a spirit of research and inquiry, which might develop some very interesting matter, and in this view, Mr Editor, I have taken the liberty of troubling you with this rather lengthy and questionably important communication from this far off land.

Response from Mid-Kent

Sir, - It is with very much pleasure that I always read the notes on olden times by your correspondent, S. W. Viney, and in your last issue I find an article with the above title, in which he alludes to Tenterden Steeple being the cause of the Goodwin Sands, he in one instance quoting a legend of an old man, who, because the Goodwin Sands and Tenterden Steeple both appeared about the same time, that the one must be the reason of the other; and, again, that the revenues which should have kept up the groin, &c., were expended in the building of the other.

Belonging, as I do, to a Tenterden family, the only history that I ever heard of it was the contractor whose duty it was to keep in repair the groins, &c., was the same person who was building Tenterden Steeple and Church, and when he was informed that the sea was encroaching, postponed the repairs to complete the steeple, being bound for time, and when at liberty to go it was too late, as another storm had swept the property away. Thus, as I have been informed, arose the saying that "Tenterden Steeple was the cause of the Goodwin Sands."

MID KENT

In Jest

Sir, – I observe that a correspondent, ("Mid-Kent," has misapprehended me and accepted *au serieux* what was only intended ironically, and goes about to show the probability of there being some actual connection between the Goodwin Sand and Tenterden Steeple. I regret that I cannot follow him in his theory about "the same contractor" having the building of the steeple and the construction of the "groins"? What groins? Evidence is entirely wanting of any "land" in its general acceptation ever having existed, and as to the name "Goodwin" having been given to them, in my opinion it goes for nothing in the direction of establishing them as the "submerged estate of Earl Goodwin." Clearly, there is nothing in history to afford colourable pretext for believing that the sands existed in Caesar's time, or subsequently down to a comparatively recent period, say four or five centuries. If the reef, or ridge, along and above which the Sands now collects were in existence at all in those early days they would have then been too much below the surface to have interfered with the light-draught vessels of the period – mere boats; but it is quite within the possibilities that some great commotion of nature, an earthquake or upheaving of land, developed the line of reef or rocks which I contend form intermittently the basis of the sands lying north and south, or thereabouts, from the Varne, through the Ridge, the Goodwins, Knock, Galloper, Scroby, &c., and probably destroyed the projecting Headland, the Foreness, at the same time, the deposition of sand about them being a natural result, and thus brought them into very unpopular notice as a source of danger. I find that I unintentionally described the "reefs" referred to as of chalk. I should have written "schist," a primary rock, or even some harder geological formation.

Referring to the names by which they are known, accepting history as correct, this same Earl Goodwin was but one removed from a pirate or sea robber, and in those early times when might was right, and the daring deeds and shameless villainies of successful – because powerful – depredators won the applause of the masses, it may be the name was given by way of compliment to the burly sea robber, or, to be more casuistic, it may have been in bitter comparison that both the Earl and the sands were dangerous sea robbers.

Still, to the optimist, there is ever a bright side to everything, and while we recognise the dangerous character of the sands on the one hand, we must fairly admit the fact that all dangerous as they are, they form a natural breakwater to a more or less secure roadstead, and the number of vessels lost on them forms but a small proportion to those protected by them, and with the aid of good reliable guides and lights, with careful skilful pilotage, it is a moot question whether they should be looked upon as a blessing or a curse.

Ryan's riposte

Sir, - In answer to your correspondent from the antipodes, I beg leave to inform him that Stephen Wheatley, who wrote England's Gazetter in the 27th reign of George II, received a very flattering letter from the Right Hon. Arthur Onslow, the speaker of the House of Commons, for his accuracy in his description; in fact, it has been taken as evidence in Courts of Law in cases of trusts and endowments for charitable and educational purposes, and even in titles of succession. As regards his account of the Goodwin Sands, the same has been verified by Camden, Leyland, and Toland, i.e., that the Abbot of St Austin's Monastery, at Canterbury, was so eager to complete Tenterden Steeple that he neglected the sea-wall, and the sea broke in and drowned the land, leaving it covered with sand.

J. R. Ryan

Sand banks – their origins, uses and demolition

Sir, – I observe that my lucubration, *re* the above dangerous sands, which you did me the honour to publish, has induced the attentions of other contributors. They, however, although severally citing different authorities, produce identically the same story told by the old man to the commissioner, Sir Thomas More – without any disrespect intended towards them – a cock and a bull story about "Tenterden Steeple." This might have been accepted in those early times, but in these days of enlightened thought I trow we must have a more feasible explanation than the story about the Abbot and the misdirection of the funds.

There can be no doubt that the chalk cliffs now rearing their bold heights on either side of the Channel at one period in prehistoric times formed the bottom of a vast basin of marine deposit, and their present position was caused (in some of the grand convulsions to which our globe has been evidently subjected in the past ages) by the upheaval or protrusion of a ridge, comb, or reef of the primary stone or earth's crusts, and if the reader will follow the idea of the bottom of a plastic basin being upheaved by the elevation of a line of rock running in a polar direction they will observe that the natural result has taken place, and the plane of the assumed chalk basin is altered and slopes inland; and, without attempting to be prophetic, I am prepared to assert, in support of my view that the sub-channel bore will, if carried through, strike new country, not chalk, but primary rock, whenever they intersect an imaginary line running from the Varne to the Goodwin Sands, as I maintain that *all* those sands which lie nearly north and south are merely collections of sand on or round the outcropping reef of rock above referred to. These sands I hold to be practically removable, and with this view have laid my views before the Trinity Board, and am still in correspondence with that body on the subject.

We in the present day on land compel the rugged (natural) surface of our globe to our will and convenience; we grade our roads, cut down or bore through hills, and generally there seems nothing impossible for engineering skill and enterprise to accomplish. Why then should these dangerous obstacles be left? If a heap of stones or other natural obstruction presents itself as a serious inconvenience or source of danger, we do not go about to hang it round with lights and beacons in perpetuity, we remove it, and why not some movement in reference to the dangerous accumulations which we know as sands? If any of your readers, nautical men, will take down their chart to the Channel and North Sea, they will find that a nearly north and south line will intersect longitudinally the following "Sands": The Varne, Ridge, Goodwin, Knole, Knock, Galloper, and so on to the sands at the back of Yarmouth roads; and I have no difficulty in my own mind in recognising each sand as the locality of a higher outcrop of reef or comb (quite as we see a ridge rise and fall on land) which forms a mere effective *nucleus* for the attraction, collection, and aggregation of the sand and thus what may have been merely a ragged comb only a few feet above the surface of the bottom surrounded by sand becomes the continuous depository of gravitated matter till a perfect cumulus is raised far above the ordinary level, and thus is perilous to the mariner. These I argue are removable in obedience to the sovereign will and intelligence of man, and as included in the category of public dangers. The subject, however Utopian it may appear at first sight, should receive fair consideration. I would not be in favour of disturbing the Goodwins or the Yarmouth Sands. All dangerous as they are on the one hand to the few, they form grand protective roadsteads to the many on the other.

In a future paper I may propound another and, right or wrong, a very interesting theory in relation to the Brake Sand which your nautical men will tell you it is a misnomer to term a sand, as it is really a heap of stones more or less rounded by attrition or other causes – of which, however, more hereafter.

I trust I may not be misunderstood as in any wise offensively repudiating the funny old-time tradition, but it will be seen that there is a broadness of speculation in other portions of the narratives cited which show that the writers drew largely on imagination, and were clearly somewhat at sea as to their facts. Ireland, in his history, says "Goodwin owned much flat land in the eastern part of this parish (Tenterden), near the Isle of Thanet," the nearest points of the respective localities being between 20 and 30 miles apart. And the writer of *England's Gazetteer*, quoted by Mr Ryan, certainly never went on foot from Margate to Dover, or he would have been unpleasantly aware that twelve miles would leave him far short of his intended goal. With these glaring blunders before one it is hardly to be wondered if we accept their quoted tradition about the probable cause of the Goodwin with some hesitation or doubt. That these great convulsions have occurred, and still occur, to alter the physical character of the earth from time to time, *teste* the volcano and subsequent subsidence in the Straits of Sunda, and the well authenticated appearance and sudden disappearance of an island in the Mediterranean, and it is to some great convulsive re-arrangement of the broken up earth-crust that we must look for the *raison d'être* of the upheaval and disruption of a palæoeval ocean bed (chalk), and the appearance of the primary rock in places the which have formed the *nuclei* of the various sands.

I commend my theories to the notice of any who have made geology a study, and should they find from competent authority that any of my deductions or speculations have any basis, it might be worth while to give the subject some careful consideration, and we do not know what beneficial results – either in a practically utilitarian sense or mere scientific and interesting discoveries – might be evolved.

The Brake Sand

Sir, - In reference to submarine matters and their causation all theories and views must be to some extent speculative, and hence I submit with much deference my opinion in regard to one of the most dangerous obstacles of the narrow seas: that it is distinctly different in character to the other lines of sands lying mostly north and south, the Brake being an isolated sand with a base of stones, i.e., more or less rounded by attrition and the action of water. The basis of the line of sands and those lying in line north and south will, no doubt, be found to be distinct reefs or combs of schistox rock, but in the case of the Brake it would appear that the substratum of the sand is a hill or collection of stones, and of a character totally distinct and different to any stone found in the locality – indeed, for a radius of some hundred miles around the North Foreland, the only stone found is the flint, which is more or less associated with or generally found in chalk, and the beaches of the locality are composed of disintegrated and water worn pieces of that stone.

It then becomes a question how and whence came this collection of - so to speak – "foreign" stone where we now find it? We cannot conceive any convulsion of nature could have so deposited in one compact heap, as, for the sake of argument, if we say it was the result of volcanic action – if there were any evidences of such forces having ever existed in the locality – the stone would have inevitably been cast out broadcast, and must *a priori* have been accompanied by some form of lava or conglomerate. All such, however, are only noticeable by their absence, and we must cast about further for speculative solution of the puzzle, and I very differentially but firmly submit the possibility of its being the result of glacial action, and that the Brake Sand is really a gathering of sand around and over the *moraine* of some vast glacier, which, sliding slowly down some ravine in the icy north, floated southward to northern Britain, and drifted southward, got set in the embouchure of the Thames, and being caught in the strong race which must have run through (on the ebb) between the Isle of Thanet and the main land of Kent, and so rushed out into the little Downs or Pegwell Bay, and it is not too extravagantly speculative to imagine that it would drift across to the eastward till it probably shoaled and grounded on the Goodwin or the reef which now forms their backbone, the warmer waters coming in from the ocean (the Atlantic), would very probably hasten its decomposition or thawing, and the stones which it contained locked up for ages in its icy fold would naturally fall to the bottom, and nor tide nor sea action would remove them, the sand would gather round and over them and *voila tout*.

Perhaps this may at first sight be accepted as a rather bold and questionably well-based theory, and I shall, in contravention of the axiom "give your decision but never offer your reasons therefore," proceed to explain some of the grounds on which I base the above theory. The stone found on this sand is, I am credibly informed, chiefly what is known as "volcanic mudstone," which really means mud thrown out by some ebullient volcano or geyser, and cooling in its descent into more or less spheroid form (in a similar manner to molten lead dropped from a height cools into round form or shot). At any rate, we find this to be generally the case with Basalts or vesicular stone which has been ejected from any volcano.

My attempt at marking out the course of the iceberg or glacier has, I take it, something like a warranty in the fact that stone which are, I believe, nearly identical in character with those forming the Brake were, and I daresay are still, dredged up by the Colchester oyster boats, and as they had a certain specific commercial value were always conserved, being subsequently kilned and made into a very valuable cement – in fact, possessing the best properties of gypsum or lime. I conceive that these stones so found on the Essex coast dropped from the mass as it drifted along gradually thawing at the edges as it came south. If my theory holds water, and the stone of the Brake does possess any commercial value, I should suppose it would require but little persuasion to induce business people to enter on the business of raising the stone for the purpose of converting it into a marketable article, and at the same time removing a very dangerous stumbling block from one of the most intricate pieces of channel navigation.

It is a question which I submit with respectful deference whether it would not answer the purpose of the Trinity Board – having tested the stability or otherwise of the premises I put forth by the procuring of some of the said stone and submitting it to the analysis and experiment of some scientific expert or practical cement maker, and thus ascertaining the value (if any) of the stone – to remove the stone and dispose of it, or issue permission to remove it on a royalty, the returns from which would probably be very considerable and sufficient to do some other sub-marine "grading."

Volcanoes, glaciers and icebergs

Sir, – I fear that this paper will only have a partial interest for the majority of your readers outside the mariner or geologist, although I am proud to believe that it is within the limits of possibility that there may be some undertie of practical utility. In my letter *anent* the Goodwins (which you were kind enough to publish) I stated I might have something to say about the Brake Sand, *le voilà!* To those who go down to the sea in ships or boats it will be no news to learn that the Brake Sand is a sand on the *locus a non* principle being more a heap or collection of stone boulders of large size, more or less rounded by attrition. Of course, some sand collects around them, but it is more a heap of stones than a sand. I then venture the opinion that this collection of stone is the result of glacial operation, in fact is a "Moraine" pure and simple. I think I have in some former letters shown that within historic time there was an open channel between Reculvers (Regulbium) on the north, and Richborough (Rutupia) on the south side, as the older writer says –
"Mari profundo Rutupinis prosim,"
and I theorise a huge glacier breaking away from the frozen north during the summer months, and after bumping along the north-eastern coast and the Essex flats, sucked through the then open channel (now Minster Level), and striking on the north end of the Goodwin, gradually deliquescing under the combined influences of summer heat and the warmer waters from the Atlantic, the stones which had been part of the vast congregation falling to the bottom and forming the

nucleus of what is known as "The Brake." It may be that my assumption of the track followed by the ice island I have shadowed out may be traversed. Here are my grounds for the idea. For years the Colchester men dredging for oysters on the shallow flats and channels, generally recognised as "the Swin," picked up *inter alia* boulders of a flattened kidney shape, red or liver-coloured, a species of volcanic mud-stone which was of sufficient commercial value for them to be saved (and sold to cement makers). These stones were of a totally different character to anything procurable within hundreds of miles of the locality, and it goes without saying *must* have been brought there, and if your readers will follow my hypothesis they will have no difficulty in seeing with me that as the mass came south the disintegration by thawing – as the mass floated back and forth under the influence of the tides – went on and the stones gradually fell off and gravitated, to be picked up as described. In this view, I do not hesitate to declare that a mine of wealth (in stone capable of being made, by skilful calcinations, into the finest cement) lies at your very doors untouched but open to all. To anyone of enterprise it might be worthwhile to go out any fine day to the brake – a couple of hours sail – get some of the component stone, and submit it to those who make cements or are engaged in the manufacture of earthenware or china; the speculation of such a test would, in view of the public beneficial results, be a very mild one, and in all earnest I commend the matter to the serious consideration of some of your readers, and I shall be heartily glad to learn that an experiment has been made with, I trust, a successful result.

The only stone to be found in the chalk locality of Thanet or the southeast coast is flint and marble (chrystalline or ??[17]) at Bethersden, so that should the stone referred to be found, on inspection, to be of a different character to the only known local deposits of formation, we may reasonably conclude that my theory holds water, and that these stones had been thrown out by some northern volcanic disturbances and been brought south and deported by glacial (or iceberg) agency, as I have indicated. Thanking you by anticipation for the insertion of my rather long paper.

Alcohol, elections, memorial poems

You have no doubt a considerable amount of interest in this new world, more especially as to our social position, and sequentially our future. At the present time the best friends of the people have succeeded in awakening the Government of the hour to the necessity of legislation to minimise our hospitable proclivities, or not to put too fine a point on it, our drinking habits, the results being the introduction of a Licensing Bill, having for its object the lessening of the number of public houses by local option, the prohibition of barmaids, and the prevention of limitation of Sunday trading in liquor, the general issue being – shall the majorities have the right of repressing the vice or disorder of the minorities or not? Of course the publican interest, including as it does publicans, owners of public house property, brewers, gin spinners or distillers, and those who import this kind of merchandise,

---

[17] illegible: looks like ?n?ri?titic

form a rather strong party, who care very little for the social or moral conditions of a people so the trade be brisk and remunerative as far as they are individually concerned, and the statistics of the various gaols, hospitals, lunatic asylums, and coroner's inquests form but very unimportant factors in *their* calculations. The masses, however, *do* consider these matters, and the axe will most assuredly be laid to the root of the tree, and although they have passed the Bill in a merely emasculated form for the present, the coming General Election will enable this question to be subjected to a crucial test at the electoral urns.

The Trades Unions, in their first growth a laudable dealing between employer and employees, are beginning to develop the cloven foot of the designing wire-pullers, a lot of self-serving agitators who fatten on the gullibility of the working man, and care little about the protection of the working man so that they (the bell-wethers) make *themselves* important in the form of a political power or influences. I think it is probable that the working men, generally pretty-shrewd and sagacious as a whole, will sooner or later open their eyes to the fact that they are being made cat's-paws of by the designing monkeys who now pose as their leaders or representatives.

We are as usual somewhat overdose with missionary folks, all anxious to obtain funds to go cock-horsing about the world – generally first-class I notice – proselytising and evangelising. I regret to have to say I would point out to these no doubt well-meaning persons some slummeries in our very midst, which badly want air, light (spiritual and natural), and a few bars of soap. Still far off hills are ever greenest.

No one can entertain a higher respect than myself for that grandest type of civilisation – respect for the dead, and the affectionate treasuring up the memory of the dear ones whom inexorable death severs from us. I can tolerate elegiac poetry on a tombstone, and even the much hackneyed.

> "Affliction sore long time he bore,
> Physicians were in vain," &c.

There is a quaint homeliness about it, to say nothing of the shrewd home-thrust at the medical profession, but we have fallen into a habit of tagging a bit of "poetry" onto almost all obituary notices in the papers, and, perhaps (barring the poetry), a pretty style of "In Memoriam," by publishing an obituary notice on each anniversary of the deceased. Some of these – the majority indeed – are very stereotype in their vapid stupidity, and, while they may make the thoughtless laugh and cause the judicious to grieve, I am firmly persuaded from their general family likeness that they are nearly all by one talented hand, who must be going round amongst the bereaved.

Democracy, bishop, cricket, politicians

By a Native of Margate

Assuming that many of your readers have a direct and personal interest (and almost all must have a general interest), in this young Britain, I submit from time to time a *précis* of how we live and have our being, more especially as we may be said to be working out social problems, the results of which may have some beneficial results to the other communities of the world.

We occupy, perhaps, the most anomalous of positions, for while we are certainly second to none in point of personal freedom, in no country is social law and order better respected, and, while living in the most latitudinarian democracy, which enables the bootblack of today to hold high political position tomorrow, there is a very marked and distinct underlie of Conservation apparent; in fact, almost *all* here, less the dissolute and thriftless, have nothing to conserve in *esse* or *posse,* and hence the feeling. This was admirably exhibited in the late General Election. Our trades have formed a grand and really concrete union, ostensibly for protection purposes; but some of the more crafty of the leading men saw their way, or thought they saw their way, to representative positions (we pay our parliamentary representatives £300 per annum), and stood a fair chance of attaining their end until one, the prospects of success having dulled the natural instincts of caution, exposed too much of his views by an open expression of sympathy with the late rioters of Trafalgar Square. The Conservatism of the masses was aroused – and the three "trades" representatives were duly relegated to their original obscurity, having learnt a useful lesson to the effect that we are as a matter of policy, apart from other and higher influences, abiders of law and order, and I am inclined to believe that any demagogue who may carry his propaganda of misrule and disorder is likely to find, if the people are in a serious mood, that lamp posts are suggestively near at hand.

The Anglican Bishop of Moorhouse is leaving us, suffering a translation to the see of Manchester, and I don't think that ever a man left these shores accompanied by so much sincere respect for, and regret at his leaving, as this fine practical-minded Christian gentleman, who has during his stay amongst us, by his steady course of earnest utility and the avoidance of contention, compelled the admiration of all classes, and even the warring sects have been constrained to one unity of feeling, one general wish for his future welfare.

We are sending you home another Australian team of cricketers, and it is to be hoped that some of the comments in reference to former teams may have good effect, and that the present intended company may, while exhibiting a laudable interest in the manly game, be careful not to expose the mammon of greed after gate money. Cricket, when reduced to the level of mere showman business – a mere matter of £. s. d. – loses its charm, and will eventually only present attraction to the bookmaker and those *pecuniarily* interested in the gathering of crowds, and who care little whether it be a dog-fight or a grand exhibition of manly prowess and skill so long as it swells the receipts at the gate. You will have the pleasure of seeing some new players this time, some of the old performers, who, in even the opinion of their own friends, "lagged superfluous on the stage," having been gracefully "retired."

Of our fondness for out of door sports, or to be critical, the fondness of the native Australian for these pastimes, I cannot do better than to quote some of the expressions of one of our late M. P.'s left out in the cold at the late General Election. Of course, as the discomfited gent was posing as a martyr to popular ingratitude, some little allowance may be made for his possible jaundiced views; there is, however, "something in it." Mr Mirams (a man of Kent, by-the-bye) says, "The native vote I believe, to be now controlled by the relations which the candidate bears to out-door amusements, without any consideration of any political results." As a practical corollary to this, I may say that some three or four seats are occupied by gentlemen whose main (and perhaps only) recommendations are the potentialities of nature, in the direction of football, or as promoters of foot racing, and supplying drinks to the thirsty. Singularly enough, we have two members sitting who have previously been expelled by the House for malpractices in their parliamentary positions, the country apparently having condoned, or forgotten, their "error."

We have a wholesome method in our elections – quite necessary where the attractive £300 per annum brings out every carpet-bagger, or tag-rag and bob-tail.

Each candidate deposits £50, and in the event of his polling less than one fifth of the number polled by the highest candidate of the electorate he forfeits his £50 to the general revenue. Four gentlemen on the last occasion forfeited their, or possibly their friends', money. Still it has a somewhat deterrent effect – just *pour encourager les autres* – and is sufficient check to prevent its being all candidates and no voters.

In connection with our political matters it will be of interest to you of Thanet to know that Mr T. J. Pierce, a citizen of Melbourne, but whilom of Ramsgate or Margate (Thanet, anyway), has been returned as the representative of the West Melbourne Boroughs, having defeated a generally popular candidate. So, on the principle of "the fly on the coach wheel," *we* of the little island, perhaps better known than any other of her Majesty's insular possessions, *do* make ourselves known, and make our mark, at least some of us.

Election, shipwreck, gold rush, seismic activity

By a Native of Margate

When we, in its collective sense, packed our carpet bags for this land of our adoption, we not only brought with us in skeleton our institutions but also their abuses, and, in spite of the ballot in lieu of open voting, we can hardly ever contest an election without some charges of impersonation, bribery, or treating, and so it comes that Mr T. J. Pierce, a Thanet man, whom I mentioned in a former letter, as having been elected to Parliament for West Melbourne, is now sought to be ousted from his seat on petition on the grounds of "treating," but as it is alleged it is a case of "the pot finding fault with the kettle," it is probable that it will come to nothing.

You would have heard of the wreck of the steamer Ly-ee-moon on the east coast of the continent – a sad affair, great loss of life, some grand examples of coolness, bravery, and self-devotion. A Baptist minister (Rev. W. Poole, of Brisbane), an old press friend, distinguished himself shewing he was a man as well as a Christian.

You will no doubt hear a good deal about the new gold fields at Kimberley, Western Australia, and as the *auri sacra fames* soon spreads, some of our young people may be over anxious and make a start for the new and much cracked up El Dorado. As an old digger, with the memory of many a weary tramp and much exposure and privation, I counsel any such "not to start to they get ready" – that is, in more intelligible English, do nothing rash; there is no hurry. If it is a *gold region* it will be just as good in twelve months' time. We of Victoria have on two different occasions "rushed" to alleged new fields, and in both cases the rash prospectors have had to be fetched back to prevent their being starved to death. My advice is to wait for some months, till the yield of gold is something reliable. It is in projection to at once commence a tramway from the seaboard to the alleged gold country, two or three hundred miles inland, but this will not assume tangible proportions until practical results in good substantial yields give a warranty for pushing the affair on.

We are getting somewhat remarkable this side for internal disturbances – I mean in seismological, earthquaky, or volcanic sense. New Zealand, in the locality of the hot springs, has been playing up, and in a fearful convulsion of the earth's surface locally a number of persons, Maoris and a few whites, lost their lives, being smothered in hot mud, which overflowed and swamped the settlements. Java and some of the circumjacent islands are also mentioned as exhibiting eruptive tendencies, and as the entire eastern archipelago has been noticeably subject to periodic breakings out, it is not too much to look for some disturbances in that direction; at any rate it is clear from the above facts, to which superadded the sudden falling out of the bottom of the great Kilanea volcano in the island of Hawaii, shows that there is from some cause considerable activity in cavernous recesses or the interstices of the foldings of the earth's crust just at present.

Apropos of my view expressed in a letter to the *Gazette* some time since in reference to the Brake Sand, or heap of stones, and its probable glacial or rather icebergial (to coin a term) origin, I find something like corroboration as to the feasibility of my idea in the fact that a geological party exploring Mount Bogong, in the Omeo district, at a great height, 8,000 or 9,000 feet above sea level, came on a deposit of boulder stones of a totally different character to the formations of the locality, and I apprehend that these strange stones had been deposited from some far off land by glacier, which, sliding into the sea, became a floating mass – an iceberg – and striking soundings on the then highest front deliquesced and left its *moraine*, the stones referred to.

The vicar's poem

This poem by the Rev. Gerrard Lewis, vicar of St Paul's, Margate, appeared in Keble's Gazette on 5 September 1891, a few years after Viney's last submission. Nevertheless, the contemporary Margate it describes has evidently not changed much from Viney's own "Recollections of Margate, half a century since". The subtitle "From The Danehillian" (under the title "Margate") suggests the vicar may have attended Dane Hill House Academy, possibly at around the same time as Viney.

Margate's a town upon our eastern coast,
Which they who knew it best, must love the most;
Few natural beauties strike the wandering eye –
Nought but flat fields, flat sea, and boundless sky;
A pier that holds its candle to the deep;
A tiny lighthouse where the surges leap;
A jetty, like a tentacle prolonged,
By human parasites intensely thronged,
When summer suns are fierce, and London town
By boat or rail has sent its thousands down.
Ah! Who, that sees them, can forbear a smile,
Yet with a tear-drop in his eye the while?
To see so large a multitude so gay
Drives for the time all selfish care away,
Catches the flying joy of life's brief span,
And wakes the angel latent in the man.
There is a music in an honest laugh,
Freemason's grip or moral telegraph,
That speaks directly to the heart – and then
Proclaims aloud the Brotherhood of men.

Yet Margate has its charms; the unsullied sea
Lies in its bed like cradled Infancy;
And every beam that shines, or breath that blows,
Gilds its light sleep or stirs its deep repose:
The white chalk cliffs, that line its length of shore,
Cast their short shadows on its sandy floor;
Or else, when tides are high and winds are suave,

See their own likeness mirrored in the wave:
Upon their summits spreads a world of wheat,
With larks above it, singing high and sweet;
With scattered farms, while few and far between
Small clumps of trees diversify the scene.
Here, where their fathers came, the children come,
To break the long monotony of home;
To drink deep draughts of pure delicious air,
God's gift, that lies about them everywhere:
Health to the sick and rapture to the strong,
Worthier a better bard and higher song.

In scenes like this, each hour, from morn to night,
Wafts on its viewless wing some new delight:
Once more the awakening sun, enlarged and red,
In silent glory leaves its watery bed:
Anon the stir begins; as, one by one,
Sound after sound proclaims the day begun;
But soon the hubbub, rising by degrees,
Swells on the ear and gathers on the breeze:
The ruddy milkman plies his rattling cart,
Clinks his full pail and nods to housemaid smart;
Hawkers of fish and fruit together bawl,
Each answering each, like rival cocks at call;
And every various trade sends forth its men,
Catering for custom at each Briton's den.
The British lion, breakfast being done,
Comes out with all his cubs to feel the sun,
And with a measured tread and stifled roar
Stalks down majestic to the neighbouring shore.

The sands! On Margate sands, at noontide high,
Ah me! What motley groups divert the eye!
Each has its centre, some atomic elf,
Attracting other atoms like itself;
The half-fledged preacher trying his raw hand

On doctrines he can never understand,
Plunging head-foremost – not a qualm has he –
In mysteries as deep as yonder sea;
The black minstrel in his garb so quaint,
Now like a clown and now like priggish saint,
At the same songs and capers evermore,
That keep his gaping audience in a roar;
Donkeys with riders; spinsters with their book;
Lovers whose instinct seeks some shady nook;
Children with spades, that build the mimic fort;
Bathers and swimmers at their favourite sport:
Scenes such as these, so innocent and gay,
Let gilded Fashion sneer it, as she may;
Let pride disdain them with averted eye,
And Wealth behold a bliss it cannot buy.
Scenes such as these, that make the many glad,
And show how cheap true Pleasure may be had;
That force the fact upon our sceptic view
How modest are our wants and eke how few!
Scenes such as these – alas! Too little known –
Possess a moral glory of their own,
Surpassing far the Court, the Camp, the State,
And all that mortals vulgarly call great.

The evening, and once more the brass band plays
On the far jetty 'mid the lessening rays;
The well-dressed crowds perambulate around
And drink in deeply the inspiring sound:
Meantime the sun has sunk in pomp and power,
The evanescent glory of an hour,
The happy closing of a happy day,
That fills both earth and Heaven with farewell ray;
And, as with one wide sweep the shade descends,
'Tis with a last "Good night" the vision ends.

The Margate Crier: Thomas "Toby" Philpot

…the spectators assembled to witness the departure of the steam packet at eight, the porters wheeling their high-piled loads of trunks, baskets, and band-boxes; Mr Philpot with his bell, availing himself of the numerous assembly to "bring forward his budget;" the parting shake of the hand, and not infrequently the meeting of two pretty leghorn hats for a more affectionate farewell; the ringing of the signal for starting, the ludicrous haste of many who fear to be late, the repeated "good byes" as the vessel moves from the pier, and the waving of handkerchiefs, so long as the fair wavers are visible – in short, the *tout-ensemble* is animating and delightful in the highest degree…

Don't laugh, for I
Am going to cry.

Stewart Warrender Viney

(1820 – 1897)

Stewart was born in 1820, the son of William Viney and Ann Taylor. His parents had married in St Clement's Church, Sandwich on 7 April 1811, Sandwich being the residence of Ann Taylor. On the record of their marriage William is listed as a tanner.

Although born in Folkestone, Stewart spent most of his youth living close to the harbour in Margate during the 1820s and 30s. At that time Margate was well known for its educational establishments and it appears that Stewart's parents may have lodged him in one of Margate's distinguished boarding schools, so as to provide an excellent education within what was then classed as an outstanding, healthy environment.

Stewart reminisces that his "...memory takes me back to my earliest school, somewhere on the Bank, kept by two elderly females of the strictest respectability...".

From the later content of his writings, it can be deduced that 'the Bank' was what was then known as Bankside, right opposite Margate harbour, and the two "elderly females" were daughters of a Captain Gunnel. I have however been unable to find any references to a school on Bankside. Stewart appears to have attended this earliest school sometime around 1824. Later, we find Stewart a pupil at Dane Hill House Academy, which was often referred to in local directories at the time as one of the best academies in Margate for young gentlemen.

Stewart was the son of wealthy parents. Stewart's father William, who came from a large family of six brothers and five sisters, would have inherited a tidy sum from his father Thomas Viney, a very wealthy tanner of Folkestone, but before that he had already been left a considerable legacy by his uncle, William Knight. The family's wealth would no doubt have secured Stewart a good education and freedom to pursue other interests during his youth.

It is quite probable that Stewart's father William took over the tanning business as his share of inheritance because three of William's brothers, Thomas, George and Benjamin are listed in the 1841 Census Returns as farmers in Stanford – which is about ten miles west of Folkestone. It is recorded in the 1826 will of Stewart's grandfather Thomas that the youngest brother David "…is from mental incapacity unable to take care of and maintain himself…" and was therefore left £600 in trust to support him for the rest of his days. This sum would today be the equivalent of about £517,000 if based upon average earnings. On the 1851 Census Returns, David can be found living with his older sister Elizabeth Major and her husband John in Folkestone. John Major's occupation is recorded as a proprietor of houses, so it is quite likely that David and Elizabeth's inheritance had been invested in property. William's two remaining brothers are not to be found in any English archive, so perhaps they were the relatives, mentioned by Stewart in his writings, who went off to America?

Stewart's father William must have died before 1837 because there is no mention of his death in the National Archives for Births, Marriage and Deaths that were started that year. I found Stewart's mother Ann and his sister Elizabeth as resident "sisters" in St Bartholomew's Hospital, Sandwich in the 1841 and 1851 Census Returns, but by the 1861 Census Returns they no longer appear there. Stewart's mother was born about 1784 and the only record of a death, after 1851, of an Ann Viney born around 1784 is in 1874, when an Ann Viney died in Dartford, Kent aged 90.

Stewart's sister Elizabeth was born in 1814, three years after her parents married and Stewart was born in 1820, six years after his sister. It is likely that there were more siblings, but because they would have been born before the formation of the National Archives and the first Census Returns in 1841, finding them – if they existed – may not be easy.

The early death of Stewart's father William (sometime between 1826 and 1837), would no doubt have created difficulties for his mother, so she may have thought it best to sell the family's tanning business and invest in her children by securing them a first class education in Margate – at least this is what appears to have been done for Stewart. There is little evidence of Stewart's employment in Margate after leaving education but following the death of his father, his father's friend Mr John Boys appears to have taken it upon himself to guide Stewart into a career as a lawyer. Alas, it was not to be, for the "kindness" shown by Mr Boys backfired as shown in his writings below:

"... I pay a tribute of respect to one who showed me kindness, Mr John Boys the solicitor, who, good man (a friend of my father's) gave me a position in his office with the kindly intent of making a lawyer of me. The four walls of an office were, however, too limited a sphere for me, and my exuberance of animal spirits, which, as Mr B said, "made a bear garden of the office," rendered it necessary that we should part..."

One could speculate that Stewart lived comfortably on a trust fund, left by his father for a number of years until his 21st birthday in 1841.

I have found no official records of Stewart's whereabouts in England in any archive material from 1838 onwards so I make the assumption that after collecting whatever was left in trust for him he left for America to join his cousin – whom he mentions with affection in his writings. A search of the American archives may find him there sometime between 1841 and 1852.

Stewart offers no information about either his family or any other employment in Margate, and it soon becomes apparent that he was drawn to adventurous ways of making a living, for we find him arriving in Victoria, Australia in 1852, from where he made his way to the Bendigo goldfield, engaged in digging with apparently varied success.

Australian archive sources tell us that, years later, Stewart devoted his attention to journalistic work, and eventually became associated with the reportorial staff of *The Advertiser* in Bendigo. In this capacity he gave such satisfaction to the proprietor for a period of five or six years that he was promoted to the position of correspondent in Melbourne – a post that he filled with much ability and satisfaction for many years.

In the early days of his residence in Bendigo it appears that Stewart was the hand behind *The Bendigo News Letter*, printed once a month for the convenience of Bendigonians who were writing to their relatives in England.

In about 1856, at the age of 36, Stewart settled down to family life when he wed Jane Davies, aged 22. They went on to have seven children, many of whom died young:

Stewart William	(1857 – 1857) died aged 4 months
Ann Jemima	(1858 – 1860) died aged 16 months
Ann Jemima	(1860 -?)
Lydia Winter	(1863 – 1885) died aged 22
Saint William	(1865 – 1905) died aged 40
Edith Jane	(1868 – 1896) died aged 29
Emily Elizabeth	(1871 -?)

In 1859, Viney was to essay a description of the town of Bendigo and its people, which has provided a wealth of information for historians and genealogists researching Australia's early colonists.

About the year 1873 he relinquished his correspondent's position to assume office in the Mining Department, with which he continued to be associated up to the time of his superannuation in about 1888.

Stewart never entered public life but during his long residence in and connection with Bendigo, he was a very useful citizen. He became a member of Bendigo's first fire brigade saying in his writings:

> "…We are a great people here for fire brigading, which started from a few volunteer companies in the provinces of Bendigo, the first in 1855, of which I had the honour to be an active member and officer for several years…"

Stewart started his reminiscences of Margate by sending correspondences to *The Keble's Gazette* newspaper, Margate, Kent, England from Bendigo (Sandhurst), Australia, in 1882. His last correspondence was sent in 1886.

Stewart Warrender Viney died on 2 May 1897, at Prahran, Australia. His wife Jane died in 1908 aged 74, the couple having outlived at least five of their children.

Chronology

1811	Parents William Viney and Ann Taylor married
1814	Sister Elizabeth born
1820	Stewart born
1826	Grandfather Thomas Viney left a will
1838	Last date mentioned in his writings of Margate
1841-1852	Possibly living in America
1852	Arrives in Australia
1854-1873	Journalist for Bendigo news and correspondent in Melbourne
1855	Officer of the first fire brigade in Bendigo
1856	Approximate date of marriage to Jane Davies
1859	Writes a description of the town of Bendigo and its people
1873	Assumes office in mining department
1882	Starts corresponding with Keble's Gazette
1886	Last correspondence with Keble's Gazette
1888	Retires from mining department
1897	Dies in Prahran, Australia

Viney and Turner

The artist Joseph Mallord William Turner (1775-1851) went to school in Margate, and spent much time there between around 1824 and 1846, staying in the lodging house of one Sophia Caroline Booth, set in Cold Harbour between the Foy Boat Inn and the Custom House. Stewart Warrender Viney lived just yards away for most of this period, so it is inconceivable that they did not at least see each other.

Sadly, although Viney may be featured namelessly in some of Turner's Margate paintings (one subtitled "I've lost my boat, you shan't have your hoop" shows the very game Viney describes on page 35 and 40), Turner's name does not feature directly in any of Viney's writings.

However, it is clear that Viney's writings convey a wonderful image of what life in Margate would have been like at the time that Turner was there – a first-hand written account that has hitherto been lacking.

In addition, there is at least one unmistakable connection: the 'dear old' Dr Price mentioned by Viney was actually Turner's physician for nearly fifteen years, and indeed saved Turner from an attack of cholera in 1847. Viney seems to have trusted in his skill (his 'bland happy manner rendered physic – however nauseous – pleasant'), and a leaflet celebrating the 150th anniversary of St John's Cemetery states that "Dr Price seems to have been highly regarded by the medical profession and to have become virtually the first citizen of Margate by the 1850s". Apparently his household was also a centre of the social scene, so it is possible that young Viney may also have encountered Turner there... we shall probably never know.

Margate Harbour by Turner (1824)

Sunrise – Whiting Fishing off Margate by Turner (1834)

Sources

Viney, S W, "Recollections of Margate", Keble's Gazette, 23 September 1882 – 13 January 1883 – 3 March 1883 – 15 September 1883 – 19 January 1884 – 15 May 1886.

Viney, S W / Ryan, J.R. / Mid Kent, "The Goodwins" / "The Brake Sand", Keble's Gazette, 31 January 1885 – 3 February 1885 – 20 June 1885 – 29 August 1885 – 5 September 1885 – 5 December 1885.

Viney, S W, "Australian Jottings" / "Jottings from Australia", Keble's Gazette, 5 December 1885 – 16 January 1886 – 8 May 1886 – 7 August 1886 – 14 August 1886.

Viney, S W, "A Chapter About Dogs", Keble's Gazette, 23 January 1886.

C M, "Ye Haunted House", A Legend, Keble's Gazette, 17 March 1883.

R B, "The Hooden Horse", Keble's Gazette, 27 January 1883.

A Week At Margate, 5th Ed., 1827, "Margate Portraits", pp.19-20

Annals of Bendigo, 1859, pp.52, 57, 278,

"Federation Index", in Digger, 1836-1888, p.1

"Federation Index", in Digger, 1889-1901, p.1

"Edwardian Index", in Digger, 1902-1913, p.1

"Pioneer Index", in Digger, 1836-1888, p.1

Cemetery Query Report, "First Register", (330), for White Hills Cemetery, Bendigo, Victoria, Australia.

Bendigo Rates Report, 1856-1881, pp.20, 27, 28, 98, 137, 138, 139, 142, 188

"Obituary", Bendigo Advertiser, 4 May 1897.

Canterbury Marriage Licences, 1810-1837, Vol. 34, 1811

1851 Census Returns for St Bartholomew's Hospital, Sandwich

1826 will of Thomas Viney: http://freepages.genealogy.rootsweb.ancestry.com/~folkestonefamilies/

Purchasing Power of British Pounds: http://www.measuringworth.com/ppoweruk/

Bent, fl. 1860-1891, photographer, "Viney, S W – Portraits. Portrait photographs. Albumen prints", Society of Old Bendigonians, 1853.

Edmunds, W, "Plan of the Town of Margate 1821".

Perry, W, "Dane Hill House Academy", Margate, Parker Collection, No. 1737.

Shury, J J, engravings from drawings by Captain G Varlo, R.M. in the book, *Pictures of Margate and Its Vicinity 1820*, by W C Oulton, Esq.

Other engravings from Margate Library collection

Stephen Michael Channing BA (Hons)
(1953 – and still going)

Born and raised in the East End of London Steve Channing's memories of his early childhood are of pulling girl's pigtails and of the many scrapes he got into while he explored his heavily bombed environment, rather than any academic successes. It was not until 1966, when the family moved to paradise (Margate) that he began to "grow up" and take education seriously.

Steve has been married to his wife Shirley for 36 years and has three children, Matt, Dan and Kerina, and six wonderful grandchildren.

At the age of forty four Steve gained a BA (Hons) in Social and Economic History at the University of Kent: a far cry from his normal occupation in the construction industry, but Steve had always had a passion for history and felt he needed to gain some form of credibility in the subject. It was the social aspect of history that Steve found most interesting, particularly as he had been tracing his family tree with his brother Malcolm for over 25 years. This pursuit had prompted him to research each generation's social and economic surroundings, in order to produce a book about the Channing family.

It was through the genealogy research that Steve came into contact with many apparently undiscovered historical social gems and he was sensible enough to keep a record of them. These gems included one of Mr Viney's offerings to Keble's Gazette and, as usual, Steve kept it. Months later, while carrying out further unrelated research, he came across another of Viney's writings, written two years later than the previous discovery. It became apparent that there could be more so, when time allowed, Steve made a concerted methodological search which, after several months of meticulous attention, had uncovered writings by Mr Viney over a period of four years between 1882-86. When collated, Steve recognised that what he had found was a rare, early, sociological gem that needed to be shared with others – hence this book.

Index of names, places and topics

apples, 16, 23, 34, 41, 45
bathing, 11, 12, 14, 34, 39
beer, 7, 34, 35, 42, 60
boat building, 12, 16, 19, 23, 30
Boots, 11, 32
Christmas, 17, 38, 44, 45
cricket, 62
dancing, 21, 22, 36
donkeys, 12, 13, 30, 38
elections, 61, 62, 63
ghosts, 29, 30, 45
Hoodening, 17, 37, 44, 45
horses, 16, 17, 38, 41, 44, 45, 49
Keble's Gazette, 36, 40, 64
Londoners, 6, 12, 15, 19, 25, 31, 41
music, 14, 15, 24, 38, 44, 45
people
  Adams, 27, 39
  Arnsell, 21
  Barham, 6, 7, 51
  Bartlett, 22, 40
  Bayly, 11
  Bennett, 38
  Bettison, 15, 17
  Bidder, 32
  Blain, 41
  Boys, 25, 39
  Brazier, 22
  Capp, 47
  Chancellor, 7
  Cobb, 7, 21, 34, 35, 40, 51
  Cowham, 42
  Croft, 33, 40
  Crow, 24
  Crump, 27
  Culhill, 26
  Dibden, 51
  Dixon, 10, 34
  Doughty, 22, 23, 27

  Draper, 7
  Dyason, 26
  Elliott, 16
  Emptage, 22, 27
  Epps, 27
  Faulkner, 29
  Forster, 10
  Fox, 22, 41
  Fry, 52
  Garner, 7, 12, 15, 34
  Gore, 12, 30, 39
  Gunnel, 35
  Harman, 22, 27
  Hoffman, 25
  Howe, 32
  Hubbard, 22
  Hudson, 6, 22
  Hunter, 25
  Ingoldsby, 6, 7, 51
  Jarvis, 25
  Jenkins, 22
  Jennings, 22
  Keen, 52
  Lansell, 13, 26, 28, 39, 41
  Levy, 15, 27
  Lewis, 25, 26, 29, 65
  Lushington, 22
  Malpas, 19, 41
  Mannings, 39
  Marinack, 26
  Mathews, 11, 32
  Maxted, 22
  Mickleburgh, 26, 27
  Mirams, 63
  Moore, 16, 28, 51, 53
  Nasmyth, 47
  Nepos, 43
  Newbold, 26, 36
  Philpot(t), 10, 36, 47, 68

Pierce, 63
Prebble, 33, 40
Price, 15, 25, 73
Quested, 22
Reynolds, 26
Ross, 36
Rowe, 22
Russell, 51
Salter, 12, 28
Sandwell, 22, 27, 33
Saville, 23
Sibbald, 24
Solly, 30, 33, 34, 39, 41
Spence, 42
Staner, 27
Stanley, 26
Stokes, 10
Stranach, 41
Stranack, 12, 23
Tring, 33
Turner, 13, 18, 73
Valder, 39
Vining, 24
von Joel, 21
Waddington, 15, 25
Waghorn, 11
Watson, 13, 38, 39
Wheatley, 56
Whistler, 48
places
  abbey, 36
  Albert Square, 30
  Alfred Square, 16
  Angel House, 45
  Assembly Rooms, 31, 32
  Bankside, 12, 19, 28, 40
  Bendigo, 14, 39, 41
  Bethersden, 60
  Boulevard, 36
  Brake Sand, 57, 58, 59, 60, 64
  bridge, 9, 10, 28
  Britannia Square, 16

  Brooks, 52, 53, 54
  Buenos Ayres, 6, 25
  Cecil Square, 17, 32, 54
  Channel, 56, 57
    tunnel, 41
  Channel Islands, 16, 34, 39, 41
  clock tower, 7
  Cobb's Bank, 21, 35
  Cold Harbour, 6, 13, 22, 73
  Cranbourne Alley, 25, 26, 29, 30
  Creek, 10
  Cross Street, 33
  Custom House, 6, 16, 18, 30, 42, 73
  Dane, 6, 10, 21, 26, 27, 30, 38, 42, 52, 53, 54, 65
  Deal, 36, 47, 51
  Droit, 7, 8
  Foreland, 52, 53, 58
  Foreness, 52, 55
  Fort, 6, 10, 17, 18, 26, 29, 30, 35, 44
  Galloper, 52, 55, 57
  Gloucester Lodge, 26
  Goodwin Sand, 51, 52, 53, 54, 55, 56, 57, 58, 59
  Grand Hall, 36
  harbour, 7, 10, 12, 27, 31, 36, 40
  Hartsdown, 21, 54
  Hawley Square, 11, 15, 54
  High Street, 7, 11, 12, 15, 23, 27, 31, 34, 39, 54
  Hilderstone, 15
  Imperial Hotel, 7, 12
  Jarvis's Landing Place / Jetty, 5, 6, 8, 13, 19, 20, 33, 40, 42, 51
  Jolly's bazaar, 15
  King Street, 10
  Knock, 52, 55, 57
  Knole, 57
  Levy's Boulevard, 15
  Library, 7, 12, 15, 17, 34

lighthouse, 7, 41
Little Beach, 40
Lockup, 33, 40
London bazaar, 15
Margate Roads, 41
Marine Drive, 34
Marine Parade, 9, 10
Marine Terrace, 13, 17, 23, 28, 31, 54
Market, 33
Minster, 45, 52, 53, 59
Monkton, 44
Nayland Rocks, 7, 25, 54
New Cut, 28
Newgate, 18, 19
No Man's Land, 6
Pegwell Bay, 58
Pier, 7, 8, 16, 41, 42, 43, 54, 68
Pier Hotel, 7, 13, 22
Pump Lane, 12, 30
Queen Street, 11, 33
Reculver, 28, 52, 53, 59
Richborough, 52, 53, 54, 59
Ridge, 55, 57
Royal Hotel, 11, 31, 32
Sandwich, 51, 52, 53, 54
Scroby, 55
Shallows, 10, 21, 36
St John, 18, 27, 30, 41, 52, 54, 73
St Lawrence, 17
St Peter's, 26, 36
Tenterden, 51, 54, 55, 56, 57
Theatre, 23, 24
Tivoli, 21, 22, 52
Varne, 55, 56, 57
Zion Chapel, 23
preventive service, 18, 19, 24, 25, 30, 31
pubs, 7, 60
  Crown, 33
  Crown and Cushion, 40
  Duke's Head, 7

  Elephant and Castle, 11
  Foy Boat, 6, 18, 22, 23, 34, 51, 73
  James McAdams, 7
  Jolly Sailor, 13, 39
  Margate Hoy, 19, 34
  Ship Inn, 13
  Six Bells, 30
  Walmer Castle, 25
  White Hart, 40
regatta, 27, 36
schools, 25, 26, 29, 35, 47, 65
seaweed, 23, 24, 30, 33
ships
  Adelaide, 19, 42
  Albion, 19, 35, 40, 42
  Big Kitty, 12
  British System, 34, 39, 41
  Columbine, 42
  Countess of Elgin, 12, 41, 43
  cutters, 22, 31, 34, 39
  Darling Darns, 52
  Dart, 19, 42
  Eclipse, 19
  Enderneming, 42
  Fearnought, 35
  Fox, 41
  Friendship, 40
  Fury, 42
  Gulf of Carpentaria, 49
  Harlequin, 42
  Herne, 19, 42
  Hindostan, 35
  Husband's Boat, 27
  Lord Hawkesbury, 41
  luggers, 35, 40
  Ly-ee-moon, 47, 63
  Magnet, 19, 42
  Margate Hoy, 22, 41
  packets, 41, 42, 68
  Red Rover, 42
  Royal George, 19, 42
  Skylark, 22

sloops, 41
Spitfire, 42
steamboats, 19, 20, 22, 27, 35, 40, 41, 42, 47, 48, 49, 63
Thanet, 41
Victory, 40

William, 19, 42
shipwrecks, 5, 35, 47, 49, 63
smuggling, 6, 22, 24, 25, 30
volcano, 57, 60, 64
Wales, 17, 37, 38

Other publications from Ōzaru Books

The Margate Tales
Stephen Channing

Illuminating and entertaining accounts of Thanet in the 18th and early to mid 19th centuries, with content ranging from furious battles in the letters pages, to hilarious pastiches, witty poems and astonishing factual reports. Illustrated with over 70 drawings from the time, The Margate Tales brings the society of the time to life, and as with Chaucer's Canterbury Tales, demonstrates how in many areas, surprisingly little has changed.

"substantial and fascinating volume... meticulously researched... an absorbing read" (Margate Civic Society)

ISBN: 978-0-9559219-5-7

Misadventures at Margate – A Legend of Jarvis's Jetty
Thomas Ingoldsby, illustrated by Ernest Jessop

This lavishly illustrated facsimile edition comprises a humorous story about the adventures of a 19th century London gentleman visiting the seaside resort of Margate. There he naively befriends a poor 'vulgar boy', only to have his trust betrayed...
Part of the ever-popular Ingoldsby Legends.

ISBN: 978-0-9931587-9-7

Watch and Ward – A History of Margate Borough Police
Nigel Cruttenden

A comprehensive history of Margate Borough Police from its inception in 1858 until its amalgamation into Kent County Constabulary in 1943. It covers the origins of the modern police force, detailing the influence of local councillors, JPs, solicitors and freemasons, as well as central government and world events such as the Boer War and two subsequent world wars.

This is also an invaluable reference work for genealogists or other enthusiasts researching family history in and around Thanet. Family Trees are all very well, but they do not put the flesh on the bones, and even internet searches are quite limited. Full indices make it easy for modern Margatonians and Thanetians to check whether their ancestors might have been 'involved' with the police – on whichever side!

ISBN 978-1-915174-03-1

Other publications from Ōzaru Books

The Hooden Horse of East Kent – Annotated Edition
Percy Maylam

Percy Maylam's "The Hooden Horse: an East Kent Christmas Custom" was long the definitive work on Hoodening – indeed, the only full-scale study of the custom. Maylam's original work is indispensable even now, but the first format is very rare, as only 303 copies were printed, and only a reduced edition appeared later. This new eBook includes the whole of Maylam's text, with numerous features to help those wanting to push the research further. A vital source of information for anyone interested in folk drama, including mumming. This edition also contains updated versions of the early 20C photographs.

Available on Kindle

Discordant Comicals – The Hooden Horse of East Kent
George Frampton

Hoodening is an ancient calendar custom unique to East Kent, involving a wooden horse's head on a pole, carried by a man concealed by a sack. The earliest reliable record is from 1735, but other than Percy Maylam's seminal work "The Hooden Horse" (see above), little serious research has gone into the tradition.

George Frampton has rectified this, by cross-referencing dozens of newspaper reports, census records and other accounts to build a comprehensive picture of who the Hoodeners were, why (and where) they did it, and how it related to other folk traditions. Full indices make it easy for modern Men and Maids of Kent to check whether their ancestors might have been involved, and detailed references make this an invaluable resource for social historians too. Over 70 full colour illustrations.

ISBN: 978-0-9559219-7-3

Animal Guising and the Kentish Hooden Horse
James Frost

This book builds on Maylam's "The Hooden Horse" and Frampton's "Discordant Comicals" to expand the field of study into East Kent's unique folk custom: what hoodening was, what the hooden horse is, and how it can be seen in the national context of animal guising. It covers historical records and artifacts, revival groups, "Autohoodening" performances which reimagine the old tradition in a modern context, and related practices such as the Mari Lwyd, Obby Osses, various northern beasts, and stag guising. Appendices contain the text of numerous contemporary verses and plays. Over 60 full colour illustrations, many never seen before in print.

ISBN: 978-1-915174-06-2

Other publications from Ōzaru Books

A Victorian Cyclist – Rambling through Kent in 1886
Stephen & Shirley Channing

For the late Victorians, "velocipedes" were a novelty disparaged as being unhealthy and unsafe – indeed tricycles were for a time seen as more likely to succeed. Some people however adopted the newfangled devices with alacrity, embarking on adventurous tours throughout the countryside.

One of them documented his 'rambles' around East Kent in such detail that it is still possible to follow his routes on modern cycles, and compare the fauna and flora (and pubs!) with those he vividly described. Over 200 illustrations, complemented by a fully updated website.

ISBN: 978-0-9559219-7-1
Also available on Kindle

Bicycle Beginnings
And what people of the 19th century were really saying about it
Stephen Channing

The best way to get a feel for what early 'velocipedists' encountered is to read the words of the times, and this book gathers into one volume the most enlightening, entertaining and extraordinary insights from contemporary sources.

The mammoth work (over 190,000 words, covering the period 1779 to 1912) contains race reports, legal developments, technical innovations and inventions, records, advertisements, acrobatics, clothing, poems, arguments for and against the new-fangled vehicles, debates over women cyclists, and a long travelogue, "Berlin to Budapest on a Bicycle" capturing the excitement of a forgotten age of adventure on two wheels.

Not all the inventions were two-wheeled, however. This book also reveals the numerous variations that came into being before makers standardized on the shapes we commonly see nowadays: tricycles, ice velocipedes, water-paddle hobby-horses... These are explained with the aid of numerous illustrations, covering the gamut from cartoons to technical drawings and photographs. Even the race reports demonstrate far more variety than we are accustomed to seeing: 'ordinaries' (penny farthings) versus 'safety' bicycles versus tandems, monocycles, dwarf cycles, tricycles, double tricycles, four-wheel velocipedes, horses, ice skaters, steamships...

ISBN: 978-1-5210-8632-2
Also available on Kindle

Other publications from Ōzaru Books

The Cairnmor Trilogy
Sally Aviss

Book 1: The Call of Cairnmor	ISBN: 978-0-9559219-9-5
Book 2: Changing Tides, Changing Times	ISBN: 978-0-9931587-0-4
Book 3: Where Gloom and Brightness Meet	ISBN: 978-0-9931587-1-1

The Scottish Isle of Cairnmor is a place of great beauty and undisturbed wilderness, a haven for wildlife, a land of white sandy beaches and inland fertile plains, a land where awe-inspiring mountains connect precipitously with the sea. To this remote island comes a stranger, Alexander Stewart, on a quest to solve the disappearance of two people and their unborn child; now heirs to a vast fortune.

In the dense jungle of Malaya in 1942, Doctor Rachel Curtis stumbles across a mysterious, unidentifiable stranger, badly injured and close to death. Changing Times, Changing Tides introduces new personalities, in a unique combination of novel and history that tells a story of love, loss, friendship and heroism as the characters are shaped and changed by the ebb and flow of events around the Second World War.

The final book in the Cairnmor Trilogy takes the action forward into the late 1960s. It is a story of heartbreak and redemptive love, reflecting the conflicting attitudes, problems and joys of a liberating era.

Message from Captivity
Sally Aviss

When diplomat's daughter Sophie Langley is sent to St Nicolas in order to care for her two elderly aunts, she finds herself trapped in an unenviable position following the German invasion. In the Battle for France, linguist and poet Robert Anderson finds himself embroiled in an impossible military situation. From the beautiful Channel Islands to the very heart of Nazi-occupied Europe, Message From Captivity weaves factual authenticity into the fabric of a narrative where the twists and turns of captivity, freedom and dangerous pursuit have unforeseen consequences.

ISBN: 978-0-9931587-5-9   Also available on Kindle

The Girl in Jack's Portrait
Sally Aviss

Struggling barrister Callie Martin, soldier Jamie Rutherford, divorcee Edie Paignton, architect Ben Rutherford, businessman Erik van der Waals, mental health nurse Sarah Adhabi... Six people seeking an escape from their pasts and redemption in the present; six people who find their lives interwoven and their secrets revealed.

But just who is the Girl in Jack's Portrait?

ISBN: 978-0-9931587-6-6   Also available on Kindle

Other publications from Ōzaru Books

Curling Wisps & Whispers of History
LucyAnn Curling
Vol. 1: Thanet to Tasmania

If family history is about gathering as many ancestors as possible, this book fails: it focuses on just three generations of the author's paternal side, between 1780 and 1826. At first nothing stirs the still waters of centuries of East Kent farming tradition. Men organize parish affairs, women follow domestic routines, boys attend a boarding school in Ramsgate, and only grandma seems interested in socializing or travel. Why then did Thomas Oakley Curling uproot everything and take his family on a marathon five-month voyage to Van Diemen's Land? Why leave one child behind? And where does Sir Charles Napier fit in?

The genealogical quest starts naturally with a family heirloom, but soon tangential questions emerge, as multiple threads are collated and woven into one story. 'Georgian & Regency ancestors' might sound remote, removed from our reality, but the individuals' letters draw us into their world, and copious illustrations punctuate the text, animating the environments in which they lived.

ISBN 978-1-915174-02-4

Vol. 2: Kent to Kefalonia

This second volume finds the Curling family back in England, struggling to find a financial foothold in society. Second son, Edward, has an unrewarding job in an attorney's office when Charles James Napier offers him a golden opportunity on the island of Kefalonia.

Follow the surprising twists of providence as Edward works on Napier's unusual project. What is the Malta connection? Tensions between Napier and his line manager, Sir Frederick Adam, have repercussions for Edward. Greece at this time was fighting for independence from the Ottoman Empire, and that war touches Napier's personal life obliquely but with lasting effect, while Edward's too is permanently changed by a different encounter. Edward's work journal and numerous letters in the Napier Papers at the British and Bodleian Libraries bear witness to the social pressures acting on all members of this extended clan, as their feelings come into conflict with accepted norms, and set the stage for further dramatic developments...

ISBN 978-1-915174-07-9

Other publications from Ōzaru Books

Reflections in an Oval Mirror
Memories of East Prussia, 1923-45
Anneli Jones

8th May 1945 – VE Day – was Anneliese Wiemer's twenty-second birthday. Although she did not know it then, it marked the end of her flight to the West, and the start of a new life in England.

These illustrated memoirs, based on a diary kept during the Third Reich and letters rediscovered many decades later, depict the momentous changes occurring in Europe against a backcloth of everyday farm life in East Prussia (now the north-western corner of Russia, sandwiched between Lithuania and Poland).

ISBN: 978-0-9559219-0-2   Also available on Kindle, and in German

Carpe Diem
The Ongoing Journey of an East Prussian Exile
Anneli Jones

This sequel to "Reflections in an Oval Mirror" details Anneli's post-war life. The scene changes from life in Northern 'West Germany' as a refugee, reporter and military interpreter, to parties with the Russian Authorities in Berlin, boating in the Lake District with the original 'Swallows and Amazons', weekends with the Astors at Cliveden, then the beginnings of a new family in the small Kentish village of St Nicholas-at-Wade. Finally, after the fall of the Iron Curtain, Anneli is able to revisit her first home once more.

ISBN: 978-0-9931587-3-5

Skating at the Edge of the Wood
Memories of East Prussia, 1931-1945… 1993
Marlene Yeo

In 1944, the thirteen-year-old East Prussian girl Marlene Wiemer embarked on a horrific trek to the West, to escape the advancing Red Army. Her cousin Jutta was left behind the Iron Curtain, which severed the bonds that had made the two so close.

This book contains dramatic depictions of Marlene's flight, recreated from her letters to Jutta during the last year of the war, and contrasted with joyful memories of the innocence that preceded them.

Nearly fifty years later, the advent of perestroika meant that Marlene and Jutta were finally able to revisit their childhood home, after a lifetime of growing up under diametrically opposed societies, and the book closes with a final chapter revealing what they find.

ISBN: 978-0-9931587-2-8   Also available on Kindle, and in German

Other publications from Ōzaru Books

Sunflowers – Le Soleil
MURAI Shimako
A play in one act, translated from the Japanese by Ben Jones

Hiroshima is synonymous with the first hostile use of an atomic bomb. Many people think of this occurrence as one terrible event in the past, which is studied from history books. Shimako Murai and other 'Women of Hiroshima' believe otherwise: for them, the bomb had after-effects which affected countless people for decades, effects that were all the more menacing for their unpredictability – and often, invisibility.

This is a tale of two such people: on the surface successful modern women, yet each bearing underneath hidden scars as horrific as the keloids that disfigured Hibakusha on the days following the bomb.

ISBN: 978-0-9559219-3-3

Ichigensan – The Newcomer
David Zoppetti
Translated from the Japanese by Takuma Sminkey

Ichigensan is a novel which can be enjoyed on many levels – as a delicate, sensual love story, as a depiction of the refined society in Japan's cultural capital Kyoto, and as an exploration of the themes of alienation and prejudice common to many environments, regardless of the boundaries of time and place.

Unusually, it shows Japan from the eyes of both an outsider and an 'internal' outcast, and even more unusually, it originally achieved this through sensuous prose carefully crafted by a non-native speaker of Japanese. The fact that this best-selling novella then won the Subaru Prize, one of Japan's top literary awards, and was also nominated for the Akutagawa Prize is a testament to its unique narrative power.

ISBN: 978-0-9559219-4-0   Also available on Kindle, and in German

The Body as a Vessel
Approaching the Methodology of Hijikata Tatsumi's Ankoku Butō
MIKAMI Kayo
An analysis of the modern dance form
Translated from the Japanese by Rosa van Hensbergen

When Hijikata Tatsumi's "Butō" appeared in 1959, it revolutionized not only Japanese dance but also the concept of performance art worldwide. It has however proved notoriously difficult to define or tie down. Mikami was a disciple of Hijikata for three years, and in this book, combines insights from these years with earlier notes from other dancers, to decode the ideas and processes behind butō.

ISBN: 978-0-9931587-4-2

Other publications from Ōzaru Books

Courtly Feasts to Kremlin Banquets
A History of Celebration and Hospitality: Echoes of Russia's cuisine
Mikami Oksana Zakharova and Sergey Pushkaryov
Translated & adapted by Marina George

This is a book not only for lovers of food but also for those with an appetite for adventure and a thirst for the discovery of exciting gastronomic delights.

Russian history presents us with a rich tapestry of extravagant ceremony, characterized not only by the magnificent grandeur of individual courtly feasts but also by successive generations of nobility actively vying with each other to surpass the splendour created by their predecessors. Russian hospitality has always exuded a special vitality and sense of warm-hearted sociability. In Old Russia there was also a significant link between hospitality and the teachings of the Orthodox Church.

The political and social history of Russia has seen some very violent changes. The more shocking the political events of a country, the more brutal the cultural changes can be. At times, the differences between the past and the present are so extreme that one is faced with completely different worlds. Despite dramatic and often heart-breaking upheavals, we do surely have a duty to remember those distant roots that helped to nourish the present.

"*Modern society contemptuously dismisses and sneers at the former way of life and deliberately breaks any connection with the past, which would always have been held to be so dear at the time.*" These words of writer, historian and theatre critic Yevgeny Opochinin were published in 1909 before the full horror of the revolutionary upheaval. The relevance of such remarks is surely as valid now as then.

Throughout history, special events have been an important way of imparting tradition from one generation to another, and symbolic meanings can still be found, if one knows the stories from the past. One just has to know where to look.

ISBN: 978-0-9931587-8-0

www.ingramcontent.com/pod-product-compliance
Lightning Source LLC
Chambersburg PA
CBHW071834290426
44109CB00017B/1820